LIBERATING YOUR LIFE AFTER BREAST CANCER

LIVE FEARLESSLY

EMILIA DAUWAY MD

Dear reader,

Thank you for picking up this book and having the curiosity to open it. Maybe you found the cover or title interesting. Something caught your eye. I wrote this book so the information within reaches the people who need it most. If you decide to continue reading and make it through the book, I hope that some, if not all, of it resonates with you. The book is intended to be read slowly – maybe even as slow as a section a week. I want you to take small bites, think about and digest it. I hope you write your thoughts and reactions in the margin of the pages. Let me explain further with a story.

In *The Art of Living*, S.N. Goenka tells the story of 'swimology', which starts with a very educated young professor conversing with an old man while on a ship. The old man is very impressed with the young professor's knowledge of geology, oceanography and meteorology. The old man is uneducated and so knows very little of the theory of these subjects, despite living on the earth, working on the sea and experiencing the weather daily. The old man starts to feel that most of his life had been wasted. But then the ship hits a rock and starts to sink, and the old man asks the young professor if he knows 'swimology' (along with all the other '-ologies' he knows). But the young professor does not know how to swim. The old man, saddened, says, 'Well, surely you have wasted all of your life'.

The moral of the story is you may read and study books on swimming, but if you don't ever enter the water, you will never learn to swim. I do not want you to just read this book. Rather, I want you to experience it. If you learn something that provides a healing, I have achieved what I had hoped. I wrote this just for you. But if you know someone else who may benefit by just a few of the following words, write your name in the pages and please give them your book. Pass it along and let them know they are not forgotten.

Emilia

First published in 2020 by Emilia Dauway

© Emilia Dauway 2020

The moral rights of the author have been asserted.

All rights reserved. Except as permitted under the *Australian Copyright Act 1968* (for example, a fair dealing for the purposes of study, research, criticism or review), no part of this book may be reproduced, stored in a retrieval system, communicated or transmitted in any form or by any means without prior written permission.

All inquiries should be made to the author.

A catalogue entry for this book is available from the National Library of Australia.

ISBN: 978-0-646-80549-8

Project management and text design by Michael Hanrahan Publishing
Cover design by Peter Reardon

Disclaimer: The material in this publication is of the nature of general comment only, and does not represent professional advice. It is not intended to provide specific guidance for particular circumstances and it should not be relied on as the basis for any decision to take action or not take action on any matter which it covers. Readers should obtain professional advice where appropriate, before making any such decision. To the maximum extent permitted by law, the author and publisher disclaim all responsibility and liability to any person, arising directly or indirectly from any person taking or not taking action based on the information in this publication.

CONTENTS

Introduction — 1

Part I Sunrise: The dawning of renewed life

Chapter 1   Yoga and rediscovering the author of your story — 21
Chapter 2   Mindfulness: from Zen to Zinn and back again — 27

Part II Sunset: Reflections of the breast cancer journey

Chapter 3   Tapas that are hard to swallow — 37
Chapter 4   The bald, the beautiful and letting go of your banana — 43
Chapter 5   The great storyteller, your mind — 53
Chapter 6   Unlocking the secret mysteries of the universe inside — 63
Chapter 7   Tick-tock on the clock, the time for joy is now — 69
Chapter 8   The Southern Hemisphere: Cyclones, mud and vaginas — 77
Chapter 9   Your mindset, your health, your responsibility — 85
Chapter 10   Training your monkey with loving-kindness — 93
Chapter 11   Busy living, busy dying and no time for fear — 101

Conclusion: Steps for dancing in the dark — 107
Afterword — 115
Key terms — 121
References and recommended reading — 123
Acknowledegments — 125
Author bio — 127

INTRODUCTION

Good morning. Come on in and have a seat. Perhaps you've met me before, perhaps not. If you have met me before, in my office, you know I usually wear a dress and, of course, heels. (I love my heels.) Today is different. I'm dressed in my comfy clothes. Hopefully, you're starting to feel comfortable too. In the past, you were likely not ready to hear what I'm about to tell you. Having been through it with so many, I can imagine how you felt when you were first diagnosed. Your eyes were wide and glazed over. You couldn't seem to take in any information, because you were frightened. Your thoughts were so loud, you could barely hear the discussion of your treatment options. Your mind was full of endless thoughts: 'How am I going to do this?', 'Why is this happening to me?', 'I'm so fucking angry! I've done everything right and I've been healthy', 'How am I going to tell my kids?', 'I could die from this', 'I can't believe I have cancer'. The mind was doing what it does best, swinging from thought to thought. You let out a big exhale, perhaps said something like, 'I don't have time for this', then you paused and held back your tears.

You kept it together through surgery, chemotherapy and radiation, as well as through your regular serving of life responsibilities. But even now, after treatment, you are still afraid. Everyone else has moved on. Your family and friends speak as if nothing ever happened and that you are fine now. You have returned to work and are no longer given considerations for your 'condition'. When you do have a minor meltdown, people are confused as to why. You were so strong during treatment. You wanted things to go back to normal, right?

But you have changed; you're no longer the same person. Even your hair, although it has grown back, has a different texture, or perhaps a different colour. People, even your friends, your doctors, can't seem to remember what you looked like before. This is your new normal. When friends ask how you are doing, you say, 'Fine' and tell them that everything is 'good'. But you have a secret and I know what it is. You sit in silence behind the smile that you paint across your face, living in fear that your cancer will return. You hold your breath until your next mammogram and exhale only when the results show 'no evidence of recurrence'. The relief is short-lived, though, and then you hold your breath again until the next time.

One of your breast cancer sisters once told me, 'It feels like a door has been shut and there is no more support'. Many of your sisters suffer in silence from remaining side effects of treatment that are constant reminders of the cancer. They live in fear of recurrence, their quality of life less than ideal. Did you know that over the last 20 years breast cancer survival rates have increased? So, the quality of your life after treatment has become even more important. The experience of illness – whether it be the common cold or cancer – is part of our human experience (or some may consider it suffering). But living in constant fear of illness, or of anything, is no way to live. Fear also has negative effects on the body when sustained for long periods of time. I am writing to you so you may live fearlessly, and feel liberated to live with joy, purpose and wellbeing.

Surgeons like me merely buy you more time – and hopefully a lot of it. However, no doubt you've already realised that one day your physical life must come to an end. You have worked hard to endure treatments, and you now have an opportunity to reconsider your lifestyle and mindset so that you may identify behaviours and habits that no longer serve you. Could your experience with breast cancer give you an opportunity to live your best life ever from a renewed perspective? Could you start to consider your breast cancer as an experience that doesn't have to dictate or define your wellbeing, but is an opportunity for growth and learning, resulting in better living? Because I know another secret too! You can live fearlessly with whatever time you have remaining! A surgeon may have removed your cancer, but you have the abundant potential to save our own life. I want to offer you tools that can empower you to live well for all the time you have remaining in this life. Mindfulness and yoga do not shield me or anyone from experiencing pain or fear, but they can help you find a way to navigate through emotional pain, fear, depression and anger. They are tools to gain understanding and wisdom.

And that brings me to something else you may not know about me. I have another job besides being a surgeon. I'm a yoga teacher too. It's why I'm dressed this way today. Yes, I know it is a strange combination, but I have found that they work very well together. We are all on a journey. It is only ours to live and share occasionally with those along the way. Let me tell you more about myself so you understand how I became this 'surgical yogi'.

Becoming a holistic surgeon

> *In order to heal others, we first need to heal ourselves. And to heal ourselves, we need to know how to deal with ourselves.*
>
> THICH NHAT HANH

I didn't always want to be a surgeon. As a child, I wanted to be a geologist and/or an archaeologist. Amassing a large collection of rocks with the help of neighbourhood friends, I was fascinated with the history of the world that each rock contained. When I was eleven, my teacher Mr Hillman invited me to present my collection to the class and put them on display. I received high marks for my report, but while the rocks were on display, the entire collection went missing, never to be found. It felt as if my life's work (all four years) had been destroyed and the thought of starting over seemed daunting to me at eleven. My dreams of becoming a geologist were dashed ... just like that.

A year later, Mrs Saunders, my feared science teacher who seemed by her fashion choices to be stuck in the 1940s, had us dissecting frogs and baby pigs. Unlike some of my classmates, I found 'unpacking' these animals and discovering what was inside was exciting. Mrs Saunders enrolled me into a summer science camp at the University of Irvine's School of Medicine. My mother, a single parent and a teacher, welcomed my summer distraction. During the camp, I saw a dead body for the first time in the cadaver lab (and later that year would experience the death of my great aunt from colon cancer and would see her lifeless body in its casket). Reluctant and timid at the camp, I stood behind the other twelve-year-old students. As we were being ushered out the laboratory, I finally found my courage and poked the cold, stiff, lifeless form lying on the metal table with my forefinger. And that's when I thought, for the first time, *I really want to be a surgeon*. I loved anatomy and enjoyed working with my hands.

After high school, I was fortunate to receive a full academic scholarship to Johns Hopkins University to study science. For the most part, everything up to this point in my life had been easy. Attending college was humbling. I was challenged not only to memorise facts, but also think. There, we had to apply facts or derive them. Knowing facts was useless, unless they were applied to knowledge. It was hard. The competition at times was brutal. We weren't given anything freely and the only real support came from our closest friends. I struggled. My grades were inconsistent. One semester I would be on the Dean's List and the next on academic probation. My counsellor told me that I was an 'attractive girl' and maybe I should 'consider studying communications instead of medicine' and one of my professors told me I would never get into medical school, but that a lady in New Jersey had won the lottery twice so maybe I had a chance. I even once failed a core subject that I needed to get into medical school.

My mother called me and said, 'I don't care what you study. You can study dog walking or basket weaving, but you only have four years that I will pay for. If these are the grades you are going to get, you can return home, attend a community college and get a job!' So, after four years, I graduated and decided not to pursue a career in medicine.

Instead, I decided I was going to be a fashion designer. I figured since I was creative, enjoyed working with my hands and loved fashion I would be successful. To this day, I do not know how I landed an interview in the fashion district in Los Angeles – but confidence and vision should never be underestimated. I brought my sketches and resume to the interview. The only work experience I had was from scientific research jobs in labs while studying at the university, and from working at the movie theatre and a jewellery store in the local mall before college. Nevertheless, the interviewers scrutinised my drawings, and we discussed my love for fashion and art, how I loved to work with my hands and, of course, Johns Hopkins. When asked why I'd chosen to attend Johns Hopkins, I explained I had planned to become a surgeon, but had changed my mind. Then, smiling, they thanked me for coming, handed me my sketchbook and said, 'You should really go to medical school'.

But I still didn't think that was the path for me. At the time, all I knew for sure was that I really needed a job because my mother was not having me hanging out with friends and partying while living at home. Since I had experience working in laboratory research during college, I was offered a job in the neurology department at UCLA Medical School studying epilepsy. During my 'gap' year, I implanted electrodes in rat brains to record seizure activity and how different medications could stop seizures, and what biochemical changes occurred in the brain. During this time, one of the other researchers was applying to medical school – his eighth attempt. After several months of working in the lab, I realised great effort was involved in understanding details of disease and developing interventions to relieve human suffering – long hours of reviewing data that at times resulted in negative results. Laboratory research takes passion and dedication, and I didn't feel I could bring that to the work.

Many of my friends who'd had the courage to apply to medical school had already started. I felt intellectually lazy and like I was not living up to my fullest potential, but I also feared not being good enough. After all, I had experienced failure in college. What if I wasn't smart enough? What if I was rejected like the other researcher I worked with? Nevertheless, I decided to apply to medical school, because I didn't want to live with never knowing whether or not I could have attended. But I decided I would only apply one time – if I didn't get accepted, I would pursue a different interest. I remember one night praying to God for patience (which I have worked hard to achieve since that night), but also outlining that I was only applying once so if I were meant to become a surgeon, now was the time to let me know. I know! The nerve of me to give God an ultimatum. Even so, I was not only accepted, but also offered in-state tuition at the University of Illinois. My friend at the lab was rejected again. He genuinely congratulated me; however, I realised that I needed to apply myself because others had the desire to attend medical school and were not given the opportunity. I was so grateful.

While in medical school, although many subjects were interesting, my focus remained in surgery. My year in the lab performing procedures had confirmed surgery was my passion. And, for the most part, medical school was much more pleasant and easier than my premedical studies. I didn't struggle with my studies, but I did struggle personally.

During my first year, one of my closet friends from Hopkins, Diane, who was also studying to become a doctor, died at the age of 23. How could someone healthy and young die? How could the profession that

I was hoping to join fail to save her? How could looking at slides of liver cells under a microscope be of any use in saving a life? My doubt increased as my childhood friend's father died of gastric cancer, and then Jeremy, one of my paediatric patients at age 10 died of rhabdomyosarcoma and my eldest sister was diagnosed with breast cancer. Cancer was everywhere and affecting everyone, including those I cared about.

I came to understand the role surgery played in the diagnosis, treatment and sometimes the prevention of cancer. I discovered the field of surgical oncology, and realised I wanted to help relieve suffering from cancer. I could use my hands and acquire the knowledge I needed to remove cancer and heal patients. This was my purpose. As Simon Sinek would say, 'start with why'. This was my 'why': to make a difference in cancer care. And so I worked hard, especially in anatomy and physiology, to be a competitive candidate for surgical training.

When it came time to apply, I applied to all 48 surgical training programs and received interviews to 42, but I could only afford to interview at 13. I applied for a sub-internship at Ochsner in New Orleans, deciding I wanted to visit and experience New Orleans since I had never been. I was not expecting to be considered a serious candidate, since only one other woman and only one other African American had entered and completed the surgical training at this hospital. Still, women and blacks were underrepresented in surgery. During the sub-internship I was assigned to the vascular surgery service and the hours were long. I did well and received an excellent evaluation at the end of the month, as well as an interview. Although no one at Ochsner looked like me, I felt comfortable there. I felt like I fit in. I ranked Ochsner for the residency match program and was accepted. I did not see New Orleans again until the following year when I began the five-year, general surgery training program. I was excited and relieved to get a surgical position. However, I felt the years could not pass quickly enough, because I wanted to pursue a career in surgical oncology and that would require a minimum of two *more* years of training. Remember that I prayed for patience? Well, I was still not very patient. I was not being present or mindful, and was always living in the future, being very goal-oriented.

After New Orleans, I moved to Florida for two years while studying surgical oncology at Moffitt Cancer Center. Although it didn't seem so at the time, those were some of the best years of my life. My surgical brothers taught me how to shoot a gun, smoke a disgusting cigar, fish with a bamboo stick pole for catfish, eat crawdads ('cheap man's' lobster but absolutely delicious), waterski in the bayou swamps of Louisiana (despite the alligators) and scuba dive. In my opinion, I was trained by some of the best technical and intellectual surgeons in the country.

After completing my surgical training, I soon ticked all the boxes. The prestigious surgical appointment at a large private teaching hospital? Check. A beautiful new house? Check. New husband? Double check. Life was supposed to be grand. After all, this was success. But it didn't feel like it. It was as if I were a robot, doing a specific routine, day in and day out. The hospital wanted productivity and benchmarks met. Patients came and went through a revolving door and there was no time to connect. Although I was making a great salary, I felt like a technician and that I wasn't making a difference. My friends would tell me, 'Of course you're making a difference. You're a surgeon and saving lives'. But I felt depressed, empty and unfulfilled. Surgery, once learned and mastered, was easy to do (most of the time), but it was not easy to get the opportunity to do. Not everyone who has the desire to become a surgeon is offered the opportunity to train in surgery and not all that are offered, complete training. Perhaps you understand how easy it is to think that people don't want to hear what you are feeling or your perspective, especially if it's perceived as whining or whingeing (because, from the outside, your life looks pretty good). I felt like that. I kept my feelings and my perspective safely hidden deep inside, away from my family, friends and my colleagues – because who was I to complain about my 'success'? Something was very wrong. I thought I needed a change, and to do something more that would make a difference.

I didn't realise that I needed to change, not my environment or other people. My professional life was going well but my personal life and wellbeing were unravelling. I had gotten married later than most, so there was pressure to have a child. We had moved to a new state and bought a new home, all while my mother had developed kidney failure and required medical support. We were in a new community without family support. I went through infertility treatments that were unsuccessful, creating more stress and pressure. My fertility doctor and colleague at the hospital I was working at told me, 'Emilia, for this to work you have to reduce your stress.' I was working long hours, rounding with the surgical residents early mornings and evenings, trying to help my mother when she would call after work and take care of my home. I thought, *What the fuck?* If I could have taken a spaceship out into the universe so I could not be reached by work – or home, for that matter – I would have. I was burned out and needed a break. But I had no skills in coping with the pressure I was under, personally or professionally. During residency, I always handled pressure well, but then I'd only had to worry about myself and my work. Now I was being pulled in multiple directions.

I did what any reasonable person would do. I sold my beautiful home in less than 24 hours, helped move my mother to San Francisco and organise her new home, and accepted a job in Hawaii. Yes, I moved to paradise. Unfortunately, all my problems and responsibilities moved there as well. I call Kauai the 'Island of Broken Toys'. I met many there who had moved to paradise to improve their lives and escape the stress of the 'mainland'. And I hadn't exactly set myself up for success.

When I moved there, I had nowhere to live, my husband was still working for his company and had no job in Hawaii and my sister (having no medical background) was struggling to help my mother. One night during my second week on Kauai, a tropical storm blew through. The wind was fierce and the electricity went out. I was alone with my thoughts, without the distractions of a phone, television or a computer. Just me and my thoughts. I thought, *Emilia what have you done?! You have turned your life upside down. You are so selfish. You have moved here and turned everyone's life upside down too. You don't have a place to live and you sold your home and quit a very good job. Kauai hospital didn't have half of the resources of your last hospital.*

In a way, however, it turned out to be the best decision. I learned and experienced that wherever you go, that's where you are – meaning you cannot escape yourself. You cannot deny issues that plague you personally. Besides learning that I did not share similar values as my husband (we would later amicably divorce – well, the best that you possibly can), I began learning to be honest with the most important person, myself. I developed the professional skills to deliver great surgical care with limited resources that would prepare me to work internationally in resource-challenged areas and have good outcomes. I would go on to lose both of my parents, my home, money and my credit score – and find joy and contentment again. You and I and all beings get to experience suffering and challenges. We experience loss, pain and fear, but we rise again, still standing.

Over twenty moves, through nine different US states, my journey eventually led to Australia, where I came to understand with more clarity my purpose. I had this moment of clarity while discussing treatment options with a patient. She began to cry. She was afraid of the treatments and to die from her cancer. I realised that if I really wanted to make a difference, I couldn't just remove a cancer and send a patient back to the same conditions, lifestyle or mindset that may have contributed to their disease and possibly poor quality of life. As surgeons, we are in the business of buying time for our patients. They then return to living the exact same way, with a remaining lack of awareness, and living in unspoken fear – some of the very same qualities that can contribute to disease and death. This clarity built with each patient, and I realised a real impact I could have after surgery would be to help a person live well, through mindful living, with whatever amount of purchased time is remaining.

But I'm getting ahead of myself. Before getting into the guts of this book, I'm going to tell you how I came to be a yoga teacher.

Remembering to breathe: a surgeon's path to yoga

*Yoga does not just change the way we see things;
it transforms the person who sees.*

B.K.S. IYENGAR

Before coming to Australia, I had been on and off the yoga mat several times over the years. I had practised Bikram and Vinyasa Flow yoga while living on the island of Kauai in Hawaii, but stopped after becoming bored with the repetitive practice. After moving to Australia, I began yoga again, attending a 6 am Saturday class to socialise with friends from work. We worked in various departments at the public hospital and met for 'Yoga in the City' on the veranda at the LightBox, a wine and espresso bar. We would do yoga for an hour and have coffee afterwards. I found I was becoming more flexible and stronger, but this wasn't the only change I noticed. Because this time, the classes were a little different: every class, the teacher would speak about the philosophy of yoga, and drop in a bit of wisdom and mindfulness. So I found it wasn't only my body that was becoming more flexible. I was calmer and not as reactive in situations, and this was something I had never experienced before from my previous yoga classes.

I started looking forward to what the teacher would say to the class each week, because it was a message that always resonated with me. It was as if the message was specifically for me. Have you ever been to church and felt like God had prepared the message for you and was speaking through the minister to you, especially if you had missed a few Sundays? That was how I felt in these classes. Yoga can be sneaky that way. I had changed, and had gained an increased awareness of myself. And the physical changes also continued. After practising for a few months, one day I realised, 'Oh, wow!' My hands were flat on the floor in my forward fold or my head reached my mat in my standing wide-legged straddle. When did that happen? The more often I practised, the more I noticed about myself with a growing interest.

Later I met Tammy, my yoga teacher's teacher, and she asked me if I taught yoga too. I said, 'Oh no, I could never stand in front of the class instructing various yoga poses and speaking about yoga philosophy.' I told her I was a surgeon, not a yoga teacher.

She said, 'Of course you could teach yoga. You do surgery, right?' The more I thought about it, the more I realised I wanted to learn more about the mindfulness aspects of yoga, and then use this knowledge to benefit my patients as I had benefited. It was too good not to share with others. I had never intended to teach a class. I just wanted the knowledge and to be able to pass it on. And she was right! I was a surgeon. How hard could it be?

I decided to jump in the deep end, register and do the teacher training. After all, we had two years to complete the program. Being a bit of an overachiever, I figured I could dedicate myself and complete it in six months. I did complete the 200 hours of training required to pass level one, but it was a lot more work than just learning yoga poses. This was not an online yoga course. This was intense face-to-face training, with some people at times crying and being confronted by aspects of themselves. We learned each pose's indications and contraindications. Similarly, as a surgeon, I had been trained to understand the indications, risks and contraindications for procedures. Without this understanding and judgement, we can cause harm to patients, instead of the intended good, and yoga is no different.

We read books by Dan Millman, B.K.S. Iyengar, Brené Brown, Shiva Rea, Baron Baptiste and the Bhagavad Gita, to name a few. I started reading *Light on Life*, by B.K.S. Iyengar, thinking it was just some light reading. Yeah, right! I would sit and read one sentence, and then would think to myself, *What is he talking about and what does this really mean?* I would have to really sit and digest the content for understanding.

It is a small book but it can be read many times, and each time you can gain more understanding.

Also, part of our required reading was a series of books written by orthopaedic surgeon and yogi Ray Long, which describe the anatomy and physiology of each yoga pose. Increasing my knowledge in this area also connected with my professional practice, and I became concerned with how we perform breast surgery, and especially breast reconstruction. I realised placing breast implants behind the pectoralis major muscle (where breast tissue is not normally positioned) or using the latissimus dorsi (swimmer's) muscle to reconstruct the breast after a mastectomy could potentially cause pain or dysfunction. Indeed, a student at one of the yoga studios where I teach had breast reconstruction ten years ago and has had chronic pain since. When doing yoga poses such as planks, she now must modify the pose. I began to wonder how many of my patients had dysfunction as a result of my surgeries.

Through gaining knowledge such as this, my yoga practice has made me a better surgeon, and a more mindful surgeon. My patients have to live with the results of what I do to them, not me. I couldn't undo a previous mastectomy or reconstruction. But I could start to ask questions, approach options differently. I spoke to some of my colleagues who said their patients didn't complain about pain and dysfunction. My response was always, 'But did you ask them?' I started to find out, before I operated on a patient, what activities they loved doing, with a new focus on not only hopefully removing their cancer but also preserving function.

Coming back to your breath

Now you know a bit about my journey, but I also want to share with you what I have learned from some of your sisters over the years. If you are open to it, step on to the mat with me, and together let's continue your journey. I have much I'd like to share with you. Are you ready? Then let's begin with a big inhale in and exhale out …

Let's go back to your beginning. Let's concentrate on your breath. Your breath is a great gauge of how you are feeling and what is arising within. Think about a pleasant memory, and notice how your breath feels. No doubt, it is flowing freely. Perhaps this feels like coming back home to a place that has been forgotten. Pause here for a moment and take notice.

The first thing we did when we arrived into the world was take a big inhale in – followed by letting go with an exhalation. That first exhalation was usually loud and associated with crying. Our breath brought joy and relief to all those surrounding us. Just as our breath brought relief to others, it has been with us from the very beginning to also provide us with relief. For many of us, our breath has been forgotten; however, there is power in your breath. The yogis realised long ago the importance of breath control. Most of the science of yoga was gained through observing nature and those beings living within it. According to the ancient wisdom of the Bhagavad Gita, the breath was linked to longevity.

Pranayama in yoga is the conscious awareness of breath, and the word itself relates to life force: 'prana' means unseen energy or life energy, and 'ayama' means control of or extension of that life force. Pranayama, the fourth limb of yoga (see chapter 1 for the eight limbs of yoga) recognises the breath as a force that can both relax and energise the body, and many breathing techniques have been developed through yogic practices – for example, Ujjayi, Anuloma Viloma and Nadi Shodhana (alternate nostril breathing) – and these have been scientifically proven to increase life span.

Essentially, the slower the breath rate, the longer the life span. Humans have a breath rate of approximately 20 breaths per minute with a life span of approximately 79 years. In comparison, a turtle has a breath rate of four breaths per minute with a life span of 150 years, while a whale takes six breaths per minute with an average life span of 111 years. Animals with faster breath rates have shorter life spans – for example, a dog taking an average of 20 to 30 breaths per minute will live between 10 and 20 years.

We have the capacity through our breath to control our other vital functions. As the breath rate slows, the heart rate slows, and blood pressure decreases. When a runner has become exhausted, they stop to 'catch their breath' – to slow the breath and heart down, and to slow themselves down. Consider when you are anxious or stressed. Perhaps you hold your breath, or feel tension in the body especially in the muscles, and so restrict the flow of your breath and your life force.

Let me give you an example of this. While living in Hawaii, I was training for my first triathlon (sprint distance). I'd swum in pools throughout my life and, as a diver, I love the ocean and observing sea life, so I was already quite comfortable swimming in this underwater world. However, I soon found open-water swimming was different from anything I was used to. During one of the earlier training sessions, I was swimming as fast as I could go but was mostly holding my breath. I became anxious and tried to stop, but realised I was in too deep to stand. Unbeknown to me, my coach and a lifeguard on a paddle board had been swimming behind me. I desperately grabbed onto the lifeguard's board. They looked at me calmly and said, 'We were wondering how long it was going to take before you stopped. You aren't even really breathing!' I had not learned how to breathe for distance swimming. Now when swimming in the open water, I breathe with a rhythm to my stroke. I mentally tell myself to breathe and relax, breathe and relax, in this rhythmic manner. Through breath control, I can sustain and support myself physically and mentally. I can be calm, relaxed and fearless.

And this isn't the only area I can apply this knowledge. Learning to use breath control during surgery helps me remain calm during emergency situations, because it creates space for me to respond instead of react. And some of my patients have found this breath work to be beneficial as well. It makes a noticeable difference when they are undergoing anaesthesia, for example, and during recovery. The anaesthetist notices the ease to which these patients undergo anaesthesia, and their reduced use of narcotic medications for pain control after surgery.

Another important point is that breathing can be unconscious and conscious. Unconscious breathing is controlled by the brain stem, our primitive brain, the insula. Conscious breathing stimulates the cerebral cortex part of our brain. The cerebral cortex is more evolved and elevated. Stimulating it provides relaxation and a balancing effect on our emotions. The following mindfulness exercise is a breathing exercise developed by Dr Jon Kabat-Zinn (who I will introduce to you fully in chapter 2). Perhaps you'd like to try it now? Once learned, the exercise is a tool that you will always have to help you reduce fear and stress. Don't worry; there is no wrong way to do this. Just be curious! And remember – we are on a journey.

Mindfulness exercise: Three-minute breathing space or body scan

This is a practice that I offer my patients to help them anchor their day. It is practice of at least three minutes undertaken immediately after waking and then prior to going to bed. The body scan was developed to help provide a focus for the mind to relax from its thoughts. You can either read through the following before your first attempt, or record it to play back as you go through the exercise. Alternatively, you can go to my website (www.dremiliadauway.com) to download this breathing practice.

Start by either lying down or sitting up. If sitting, imagine a string descending from the sky into the crown of your head, and then down your spine and anchoring your tailbone into your chair or mat. Bring your awareness and attention to your breath. Realise that you are breathing in and breathing out. Notice the rise and fall of the belly with each breath, and the expansion of the chest with each in-breath.

Now see if you can allow your awareness to ride on the wave of the breath as your breath enters the inner rings of the nostrils, moves into the nasal chambers and to the back of the throat, filling the lungs and down behind the breast bone. Now let the awareness ride the wave out of the body on the exhalation. Notice the breath as it moves from behind the breast bone, from the throat and out from the nostrils. Do this a few times, allowing the awareness to stay with the rhythm of your breath.

Now allow your attention to move to your eyes. Notice the amount of pressure it takes to keep your eyelids shut. Simply remain curious, without forcing anything to happen. Pause. Notice if there is darkness or maybe you can appreciate a bit of light coming through the thin upper lid. Pause and notice. Do you see colour? If so, what colour?

Allow your attention to drift to your ears. Soften the inner ears and see if you can hear distant sounds. Then draw your attention closer and listen for the sound closest to you.

Bring your awareness to your mouth. Notice the position of your tongue. Is the tip of your tongue touching the back of the teeth or possibly resting on the upper hard palate of the roof of the mouth? Is the jaw tense or relaxed? Pause and take notice. Is the mouth moist or is it dry?

Now take a moment to observe yourself. Notice the touch of the fabric from your clothing on your skin, and the points where your body meets the structure you are lying or sitting on. Notice the temperature of the air on your skin. Is it warm or cool?

Again allow your awareness to return to the breath and realise that you are breathing in and you are breathing out. Remain for a moment longer and notice how you are feeling. Pause. Notice any thoughts. Open your eyes, and bring your hands together at your heart. Namaste.

# PART I

SUNRISE: THE DAWNING OF RENEWED LIFE

CHAPTER 1
YOGA AND REDISCOVERING THE AUTHOR OF YOUR STORY

Do you recall when you were first diagnosed with breast cancer? No doubt you were soon bombarded with stories and advice from everyone from here to kingdom come! Perhaps a friend knew someone whose mother had a mastectomy and so had decided that's what you should have, telling you something like, 'Get them both cut off, because that's what I would do.' Or someone else told you, 'Don't let them give you chemo. That stuff will kill you.' Or, 'I knew someone who had radiation to their throat, and it was really bad. They couldn't even swallow or eat. Don't do radiation!' Or, 'You don't need your breast, so you don't need reconstruction. That's just being vain'.

Do not misunderstand. I believe the hearts of these people handing out advice were in the right place, and they were trying to be helpful. However, I am unsure how someone becomes an expert of something they have not studied, practised or experienced. It's a wonder that anyone can make an informed decision instead of a fear-based decision with all the external recommendations coming from those who are fearful and uninformed.

Similarly, many myths have built up about yoga and again what is interesting is that many of the ones I have heard have come from people who have never practised and experienced yoga.

Instead, I like to follow the lead of Bhutan. Have you ever been to Bhutan? Called the 'happy country', it is a small country between Nepal, India and China, and there they have a saying: 'Take the best from the west and leave the rest'. I think that is a good philosophy. You can enjoy listening to and considering other's perspectives, but take only what is useful and leave what isn't. And this also applies to the ideas in this book. What I share may or may not resonate with you. Focus on whatever does resonate, allow it to remain like sweet residue and use it. If it doesn't resonate with you, with kindness allow it to fly away with the breeze and let it go. All I ask of you is to keep an open mind.

What yoga is and isn't

One myth about yoga is that it is a religion. I am a Christian; however, I teach and practise yoga. I believe in God and I do not worship the sun other than to appreciate the sun's beauty. I have gratitude for and love the sunrise because for me it represents God providing me with another day of life and another opportunity to make a positive impact in the world. The sun salutation is a common yoga sequence of poses that stretches, flexes and strengthens the body, and I take you through this sequence as you progress through the book. It is a sequence that acknowledges the power of the sun and the breath, and allows us to be grateful for these gifts, but this doesn't make yoga a religion.

Yoga has been and will remain universal. It is inclusive of all people from all religions, and all genders, ages, or ethnicities. It is no more of a religion than weightlifting, CrossFit, running or swimming. However, it is the only form of physical exercise that has a singular goal of self-awareness or enlightenment. I suppose you could make it your religion, but it is not the intention of yoga and nor is it a requirement to practise it.

What yoga does do is provide you the freedom to be your authentic self, stand in your truth, and explore without fear of judgement. The ancient Indian text *The Yoga Sūtras of Patañjali* describes eight limbs of yoga. Each limb – Yama, Niyama, Asanas, Pranayama, Pratyahara, Dharana, Dhyana and Samadhi – describes a different aspect of yoga to attain ultimate freedom, or liberation. (The first limb, Yama, then has five disciplines within it, and the second limb, Niyama, includes five observance of how to treat yourself – see the 'Key terms' section at the end of this book.) Yoga stills the negative chatter within the mind, especially of what others will think of us and, more importantly, what we think of ourselves.

I like to believe that my yoga mat represents life. What I learn on the mat, I can apply in everyday life off the mat. To be our authentic self, we must know ourselves. The practice of your sankalpa ('san' meaning truth, and 'kalpa' meaning vow or commitment) or intention is with you from the beginning. Your sankalpa captures your true heartfelt desires. You do not have to seek it or create it. When we are children, we live the life our parents map out for us. We learn what goals and dreams society and culture believe are important. Sometimes these are aligned with our true heart's desires, but many times we are living the dreams or life of others. When we are not aware of or forget our intentions, we feel confused and we do not live our higher purpose. Life asks us to live the best version of ourselves and have the courage to live your highest purpose for yourself and the good of all beings. What is your intention in reading this book? It is no mistake that you have chosen it to read. My intention is to introduce you to how you can use the principles of yoga and mindfulness to reduce fear and to respond to stress in a manner that supports your intention of fearless healthy living.

Lastly, one of the other myths about yoga is that it is very serious. However, yoga still welcomes humour and you cannot take yourself too seriously. As an example of this, one of the new friends I made during my yoga teaching training was a midwife. We had lots of laughs together. She was from out of town and we would stay together during the weekend-long training sessions. During one visit, she confessed that she had been diagnosed with thyroid cancer. I helped her research the doctor she was referred to and what her treatment options were. After her treatment was complete, she went for her regularly scheduled mammogram, which she scheduled to coincide with a Bryan Kest Long Slow and Deep (LSD) yoga class we were going to do together. The mammogram showed a suspicious area that was later confirmed to be an early breast cancer.

Now, you aren't supposed to eat at least two hours before practising yoga, but this called for not only a meal but also a drink. LSD yoga is a three-hour yoga class of holding poses for between three and ten minutes. We figured it wouldn't be that big of a deal. She'd had a stressful day, hadn't eaten and wanted to unwind. So we didn't have a small meal; we ordered a steak dinner and a bottle of wine. We just had a glass of wine each and took the rest back to the hotel to drink afterwards. No harm, no foul, as they say. Well, we learned during the class why you shouldn't eat or drink before class. I felt full and bloated throughout, and our practice was secretly more challenging because of the added struggle of holding in the flatulence. We were contracting muscles that were not part of the pose and trying to find steadiness and ease. There was steadiness but no ease, but we held it in. At the conclusion of class, our teacher said, 'Go home, enjoy a glass of wine or relax in a tub. Take it easy.' My friend and I giggled, since we had our little secret wine stash we'd already sampled earlier.

Again, humour is welcomed in yoga. Even some of the greatest minds in history knew that humour was important. Gandhi once said, 'If I had no sense of humour, I would long ago have committed suicide.' Laughing at myself has been an important part of my yoga practice.

Starting with the Asanas

The Asanas, the third and most practised limb of yoga in the western world, are postures used to promote a healthy body while raising awareness. Taking care of your body to the best of your ability allows for the best possible experience during this lifetime. After all, we are spiritual beings having a physical experience. Your health is your individual responsibility. Regardless of whether you believe you only have one life and then you go to heaven or you believe in reincarnation, one thing we all agree on is that this life, in this body, happens only once. This is it.

Through our physicality, we can experience ourselves on a more obvious, gross level. When you begin your practice, you have an immediate awareness of the inflexibility in your body – your fingertips may not reach your toes in the forward fold, for example. Eventually, through the practice of various asanas, the time comes when you realise your fingertips are touching your toes. Or that your arms feel longer with the hands flat on the floor. This is awareness of self. You will start to develop self-awareness through the physical practice of yoga.

Yoga has many poses and even as a yoga teacher I have not mastered all of them. I find joy and interest in realising how my body structure easily accesses some poses while others at first seem impossible – until one day my body is open to the impossible. I can learn to accept this and to respect my body in those moments, accepting it without judgement of myself. The next month the impossible may be impossible again. The asanas are a portal or invitation to learn about our bodies.

Recently, I read that self-awareness is selfish, and it reminded me that while attending a surgical conference, a doctor said that we must not teach women how to complete their own breast examinations, because doing so causes undue stress and unnecessary doctor visits. But why would we discourage anyone from paying attention to themselves? Over the years, I have had women who present with a large breast lump that went unrecognised. Breast cancer does not grow overnight. It takes years to develop. Paying attention to yourself, in the best way you can with loving-kindness, is never selfish. It is necessary and vitally important.

It is not selfish to care about yourself and try to hear what our bodies are communicating moment to moment. The question is, are you listening? And when you listen, do you hear and understand? Knowing ourselves is also about knowing our bodies. Yoga gives you an opportunity to explore your body and yourself in a different and interesting way.

As important is mindfulness, and I explore this further in the next chapter.

CHAPTER 2

MINDFULNESS: FROM ZEN TO ZINN AND BACK AGAIN

In the beginner's mind there are many possibilities, but in the expert's, there are few.

SHUNRYU SUZUKI

When you were diagnosed with breast cancer, you probably felt like the world was turned upside down. You were forced into a world that was new, full of uncertainty. And uncertainty can cause worry and fear. Is it possible to look at your cancer with a fresh set of eyes and a different mindset, perhaps a beginner's mind? With an open mind, let's consider your cancer from a different perspective. Have you heard of mindfulness? Mindfulness is often referred to in social media and books, and the term has become more commonplace. But I want you to forget what you know about mindfulness, and become a beginner again.

Remember I said in the introduction I was going to introduce you to Dr Jon Kabat-Zinn? A professor emeritus of medicine, Kabat-Zinn created the Stress Reduction Clinic at the University of Massachusetts Medical School in 1979. He incorporated the practice of mindful meditation into conventional medicine and demonstrated the physical and psychological benefits. He defines mindfulness as 'an awareness that arises through paying attention, on purpose, in the present moment, non-judgmentally'. He developed Mindfulness-Based Stress Reduction (MBSR) group programs to help patients who were having difficulty coping with life during illness. MBSR has since been demonstrated to help cultivate qualities that assist anyone with managing stress.

The diagnosis of cancer of any kind can be frightening and stressful. And we can never eliminate stress. Even happy moments can be overwhelming and stressful. Consider the planning of a wedding – a joyous occasion that creates stress as we strive to create the most perfect memorable event. So although you cannot eliminate stress, using mindfulness, you can cultivate a quality of mind that helps to respond in a manner that is acceptable.

What mindfulness is and isn't

As with yoga, many myths have developed around mindfulness. Although mindfulness has become more commonplace, a common misconception that remains is that to practise it, you must sit in an uncomfortable position for a long period of time, eliminating all thoughts. The opposite is actually the case – mindfulness can be practised in every moment. And it can be practised for small portions of time until it becomes part of the fabric of who you are. Eating, driving, interacting with family, friends and co-workers, and exercising can all be done mindfully. You have probably had moments already of practising it, without calling it mindfulness. Perhaps you have looked at your partner or child and realised a change has occurred in him or her, and you took a moment to acknowledge the change and dwell on your observation with curiosity. Maybe you have looked in the mirror and noticed a new character wrinkle on your face, or a change in the length of your hair or the colour. These observations are small moments of mindfulness, when observed from a non-judgemental mindset.

Despite becoming more mainstream in western culture, mindfulness originates in Eastern philosophy. The word mindfulness is a 19th-century translation of the Pali word 'sati'. Sati means 'memory'; however, it is not referring to memory of the past as you may assume. Sati means memory of the present, and it is a significant aspect of Buddhist traditions, and based on Zen, Vipassana and Tibetan meditation techniques.

According to Luis Felipe Morales Knight of Pepperdine University, Graduate School of Education and Psychology, mindfulness has been documented as early as 1500 BCE in Hinduism as yoga practice, in Daoism 6th BCE as qi gong practice, and 535 BCE in Buddhism through focused breath practice. The use of mindful meditation has also been found in Christianity, Judaism and Muslim religious practices, meaning it has been practised worldwide. Most religions incorporate prayer or meditative practices to move our thoughts from worldly preoccupations to a broader perspective of life, truth and reality. In the New Testament, for example, the book of Romans 12:2 (NLT) says, 'Don't copy the behaviour and customs of this world, but let God transform you into a new person by changing the way you think'. Another version of the New Testament (NIV) includes this as, 'Do not conform to the pattern of this world, but be transformed by the renewing of your mind.' Mindfulness has been practised and encouraged for thousands of years.

One of the amazing things I have discovered from my personal practice of mindfulness is I have more time. Our perception of time – that is, the hours in a day or the days of the week or the entire calendar – was created according to the rise and setting of the sun and the cycle of the moon. The allotment of time or how it is divided, however, is human-made. When we multitask without being mindful, we waste time and we do not do the task as well, in comparison to when we perform each task separately and with focus. Try this small mindfulness exercise if you do not believe me. (I did say in the beginning of the book that I wanted you to experience this for yourself and not follow blindly.)

Count from 1 to 26 as quickly as you can. Next, say the alphabet from A to Z (26 letters) as quickly as you can. Now combine the two tasks, by saying A1, B2, C3 and so on until you have reached Z26. Were you able to multitask and complete the third portion of the exercise as quickly as you completed the first two tasks separately and with focus? Usually, it will take you longer to complete multiple tasks simultaneously. The other amazing realisation is that we do this kind of multitasking every day, all day, and we are so accustomed to doing it that we aren't even aware of it. When you are really focused and have awareness, you accomplish tasks more efficiently and with better outcomes. When people ask me how I get through everything I have on my plate, I joke and say that I make time – and by that I mean that I *create more time*.

So although mindfulness has its origins in ancient practices, Jon Kabat-Zinn is considered the founder of modern-day mindfulness, with over 18,000 people having completed his MBSR programs. As evidence demonstrating the effectiveness of meditation on cognition, emotion and restlessness increased, interest grew in the field of psychiatry. In the 1990s, mindfulness-based cognitive therapy (MBCT) was developed and researched at the Oxford University Department of Psychiatry by Mark Williams. As more research was conducted, studies showed the role of meditation on emotional regulation. The World Health Organization has identified several determinants of health, including genetic, social, economic, environmental factors and our behaviours. Of these determinants, some are more in our control than others. For example, we cannot control our genetic predisposition, but our lifestyle and behaviour have been shown to impact our health considerably and these are very much within our control. Mindfulness practice has been found to create positive changes in health attitudes and behaviours. In other words, regardless of whether you adopt the practice because of scientific or religious reasons, the result of mindfulness is an inner peace and calm.

Moving away from mind-made suffering and towards gratitude

Buddha realised that through meditative practice we can reduce human suffering. Although suffering is a part of the human experience, there is a difference between natural suffering and mind-made suffering. During your lifetime, you will experience loss, natural disasters and illness. These are natural phenomena that are unavoidable. Mind-made suffering, however, arises from negative thoughts resulting in fear. (I recently heard of an acronym for FEAR: false evidence appearing real.) Of course, at times, being fearful and acting accordingly is appropriate, but fear is not a state of mind to reside in.

As humans, we are built to survive, and we still have animal instincts that kick in to help us do what is necessary to survive. We have an inherited negativity bias. However, being in fear or maintaining high stress levels result in measurable physiologic changes within the body. When our sympathetic nervous system (responsible for our fight, flight or freeze response) is stimulated, our pupils dilate to take in more light, we may experience sweating, our blood pressure increases, the stress hormone, cortisol, increases, and the functions of the immune, digestive and reproductive systems are all reduced. When you are scared, you aren't interested in eating or sex! The parasympathetic system, or our 'rest and digest' state, is the opposite. In this state, we are calm, our breath rate is slower, and our blood pressure and cortisol levels lower. Imagine what we are doing to ourselves when we are in a constant state of worry and fear, especially over things we cannot control. We are creating imbalances that may lead to disease.

In *Hardwiring Happiness*, psychologist Dr Rick Hanson writes about the significance of cultivating the good through the practice of gratitude, arguing that, through practising gratitude, we can rewire the neural pathways in the brain. Taking advantage of what's now known as neuroplasticity, we can change neural pathways as we change our thoughts from having a negativity bias to having a positivity bias.

For many years, scientists thought that the brain was a fixed organ with brains cells dying as we age, incapable of cellular regeneration. Neuroplasticity, however, was first described in 1948 by Polish neuroscientist Jerzy Konorski, who observed changes in brain cells. Other scientists then went on to also observe and study the brain's ability to adapt to new conditions caused by experiences such as injury and disease. When changes occur as a result of factors such as our environment, behaviour, or neural processes, these studies showed that we can 'rewire' our brains to adapt to the new situation. This is a process that occurs daily and which we can activate.

I know you are thinking something like, *How can I have gratitude for having breast cancer?* Many of my patients have told me that before their cancer they had the perfect life. Perhaps you feel the same. You really had no perceived problems. You were quite happy until your diagnosis of breast cancer. One of my patients had chemotherapy before having bilateral mastectomies. Afterwards, she had a bleeding complication requiring reoperation the following day. She then underwent radiation therapy. After recovering from her treatments, we started practising mindfulness. During her first session, she told me that, although she is appreciative of being alive, she had moments of depression. Never experiencing depression before and previously used to living in her perfect bubble of a life, she now found she had to deal with good and bad days. But she realised this means she now appreciates the good more than before. She doesn't take the good for granted. She allows herself to have the experience in each moment, regardless of whether it is pleasant or unpleasant, and without fear or judgement. With a new mindset and perspective, she noticed more moments where she could see the good, even in moments of discomfort.

Rick Hanson compares the brain to a garden. We sow seeds of good and must continually pull out the weeds and tend to the garden.

By nurturing the seeds within our mind, they can grow into something beautiful. Basically, our neural synapses or the communication pathways in our brain can be pruned to eliminate neural connections that are no longer useful, while others can be strengthened. How cool is that? We can use what we already have to create a healthier mindset using neuroplasticity.

Stepping back from fear

Your brain is quite an amazing organ, responsible for keeping you safe and alive, and stopping you from doing stupid things that could kill you. Within your brain is a small structure, about the size of an almond. Its name is the amygdala (which means almond in Greek). The amygdala is part of your limbic system, which is responsible for your emotions and memory. When you have an experience, the amygdala helps to process it as either a safe or unsafe experience, and to quickly decide how you should respond.

Have you ever overreacted in a situation? You know, kind of gone crazy and had everyone look at you as if you had gone completely mad? Perhaps it was a situation where even you were wondering, *What is wrong with me?* Why did I react that way? Well, to some extent you can blame your reaction on your amygdala. You were hijacked! It may have misinterpreted what was happening (based on something you'd experienced previously) and tries to protect you from experiencing the situation again. It was just doing its job, not trying to embarrass you. Sometimes the amygdala gets it wrong. Fear is an emotion that is useful when necessary, when we are threatened, but not when we are safe. When you take the time to slow down and breathe, you create space and can respond appropriately, instead of reacting or possibly overreacting.

Yoga, mindfulness and salutation to the sun

I wrote this book based on the elements and flow of a sun salutation. The sun salutation is meditation or prayer in motion. The ancient yogis believed that the body could be used to gain awareness of our higher self and that through the sun salutation practice we can receive wisdom and knowledge. This is also reflected in other ancient sources of wisdom. Proverbs 4:7, for example, says, 'Wisdom is the principal thing; therefore, get wisdom and with all thy getting get understanding.'

The sun salutation is a sequence of poses that flows from one to another, with each pose coming with its own philosophy and meaning. When one round ends, another begins. As the sun rises and sets, life begins and ends. It is a perfect cycle. These first two chapters have given you a bit of understanding of the benefits of yoga and the purpose of mindfulness. In the chapters in the next part, I explore those concepts a bit more, while also teaching you a sun salutation – a flowing practice illustrating the push, pull, ups and downs of our experiences in life.

PART II

SUNSET: REFLECTIONS OF THE BREAST CANCER JOURNEY

CHAPTER 3

TAPAS THAT ARE HARD TO SWALLOW

*Understanding is the first step to acceptance,
and only with acceptance can there be recovery.*

J.K. ROWLING

I have never met a patient who had a desire to go through surgery, chemotherapy or radiation. I'm sure you felt the same. You chose to do what was recommended and necessary to remove the cancer and reduce the probability of it recurring. You don't have control of having a cancer diagnosis, but you do have control over how you choose to have it treated. And we sometimes choose to do things that are required of us, whether it be for ourselves or others.

After diagnosis, my patient, let's call her Olivia, said 'I don't mind having the surgery, but I cannot have chemotherapy or radiation. I don't have that kind of time. My husband needs me. And I have a special needs adult son. They would not be able to manage without me.' After Olivia's surgery, she was then diagnosed with cancer in her lymph nodes, and chemotherapy was recommended. She had elected to have a mastectomy to avoid radiation, but her cancer now met the criteria for post-mastectomy radiation. She required a combination of treatments to adequately treat her cancer and reduce the odds of it returning. Of course, she was not happy with this at all, but who would be? She just kept saying she didn't have the time and couldn't have all of the treatments. So I asked her, if she developed incurable breast cancer, who would then be there for her husband and special needs son? So she did what was necessary for her wellbeing.

Much to her surprise, her husband stepped up and took care of things very well. But what really shocked her was that her special needs son was quite capable of contributing as well. She had given them the beautiful opportunity to care and support her. Now she just had to be disciplined to do her chemotherapy and radiation.

Serving up self-discipline with your tapas

The discipline required in treatment also connects with yogic principles. We all have certain things in life that are necessary for either our wellbeing or the wellbeing of those we share our lives with. In yoga, this self-discipline is called tapas, and is a part of Niyama or the second limb of yoga (and nothing to do with yummy Spanish food). This self-discipline helps us complete those things that we prefer not to do, but do anyway for our own wellbeing or for others. We may not enjoy performing certain chores around our home, for example, but we also want to have a clean and organised home environment, so we do them.

The discipline that allowed Olivia to ignite a transformation within herself also transformed her family. We sometimes tell ourselves what we cannot do, but when we have a challenge that requires us to step out of our comfort zone and face our fears, a transformation often occurs. Olivia's cancer and the required treatments gave her an opportunity to make a change that transformed her life – and her family's life – for the better. After she completed her treatment, she continued to allow her husband and son to share in the everyday responsibilities, which they collectively enjoyed. This reduced the stress and burdens she previously had shouldered alone. Eventually, she came to accept the treatments required to manage her breast cancer.

Accepting that you have or had cancer is the first step to recovery. You cannot wish it away. Instead, you need to cultivate a mindset of acknowledgement to be with the experience, as you accept what has happened and what is happening, and sometimes accept what will inevitably happen. Are you familiar with the serenity prayer? The serenity prayer says, 'God grant me the serenity to accept the things I cannot change, the courage to change the things I can and the wisdom to know the difference.' The wisdom to know the difference is as important as the first two parts. We do not have control over everything. Indeed, how much do we really have control over?

Discipline and acceptance

I too have struggled at times with acceptance. I have had to accept that I cannot help every patient who walks into my office, and even that not all of them want my help. I have had to come to terms with events and people in my life I care about who I could not help. And that I will not even be able to save those I love.

My mother passed away in 2009 from complications due to diabetes, a terrible disease. As the only medical professional in my family, I ensured she had the best possible care when her kidneys failed and she required dialysis. I recall one day, while I was performing an 18-hour operation, my mother had been calling me. She was bleeding from the arm where her dialysis catheter was placed. When she could not reach me, she contacted my husband at the time, who called the nurses at her assisted living and then an ambulance. She was brought to the hospital where I was operating, but the emergency department did not realise she was my mother, and I was still in the hospital operating. My mother had bled so much it had soaked through both mattresses of her bed and onto the carpet, leaving a bloodstain the size of a large dinner plate. She was rushed to surgery unbeknown to me, while I was operating trying to save my patient. That was one of many emergencies that my mother would have and I would be called to try to help. My mother was my rock, my role model and the person in my life I felt the most unconditional love from, but I could not save her from the years of physical suffering due to her illness, despite my medical expertise. But I could enjoy what time we had together. One of the times I enjoyed most was when my sister and I took her on a cruise ship capable of dialysing her throughout the holiday. It is a wonderful memory.

We had many ups and downs during the last years of her life, and it took the discipline of my entire family to support her during the final years of her life. Despite many struggles and challenges, I still see myself as fortunate to have had my mother live long enough to give me the opportunity to care for her. Not everyone is fortunate enough to have their parents with them into adulthood. It is a great responsibility to care for ageing parents and provide for their needs. It comes during a time of life when you may still be caring for your children, have a career and a household, while also trying to maintain leisure time to refuel and recharge yourself. When a person is facing a life-threatening illness like breast cancer, life does not just stop. Cancer has no regard for your time or commitments. Whether you are dealing with cancer, or taking care of an ageing parent or a special needs son (or perhaps all of that and more), getting through takes self-discipline, it takes tapas. It is one more thing to add into the mixing bowl of life's responsibilities.

We all have busy lives and try to multitask. We run on the little wheel that goes nowhere, trying to get ahead of the laundry list of all our 'to-dos'. Eventually we may 'burn out'. If we become more focused through practising mindfulness, we are more likely to maintain our mental and physical wellbeing and still accomplish those actions that are required of us.

The practice of mindfulness provides space to be less reactive and more responsive. Being calmer, you may start to notice what is arising within and so can start to choose how you prefer to respond in a situation, first by accepting and acknowledging it. You have more time to consider your thoughts, feelings and perspective to respond in ways that are acceptable to yourself. You're more able to recognise when something must change and consider how and when to change it. Through practising acceptance, you can start to understand that nothing remains the same.

The Law of Impermanence, also called 'anicca' in Pali, acknowledges that nothing can remain forever. It is an illusion that all objects remain the same. Everything is transforming and evolving. All situations are changing. Even a challenge we are facing will not last forever. Breast cancer does not last forever. It too will change and die. It can only live within a host and if the host does not live, then it cannot live either.

Consider the experience of physical pain: the intensity fluctuates, and is never constant. Similarly, pleasant experiences do not last forever either. Wanting something pleasant to remain, even while knowing that it cannot remain, causes disappointment. This attachment to our desires or avoidance of discomfort or pain can cause suffering – especially if we cannot accept the experience and be with it in the moment and then let it go. This can be particularly difficult when experiencing physical chronic pain. Nonetheless, we always have a choice in how we choose to respond.

Yoga pose: Mountain (tadasana)

Mountain (or tadasana) pose begins your sun salute. (You can also download the full version of the sun salutation yoga sequence from my website – www.dremiliadauway.com.)

To start, spread your awareness throughout your feet as if trying to stand on all four corners of your feet. Knee caps are raised and the thigh muscles engaged. Tuck your tailbone down towards the heels as you reach the crown of your head towards the sky.

As you find length in your spine, your shoulder blades slide down your back, creating space between the shoulders and your ears.

Place your arms by your sides as you stand strong in your foundation and your truth. Bring awareness to your breath, as you inhale in and exhale out. Close your eyes, noticing how your perception of space and time change with something as simple as closing your eyes.

Mindfulness exercise: Listing what you can control, and what you can't

Make a list of the things you can control and can change, and then make a list of those things that you cannot. For those things that are not within your control, see if you can be accepting and respond in a manner that you can live with. For example, you cannot control having a diagnosis of cancer, but you can control your approach to treatment.

Sometimes having this awareness and bringing this reality to the forefront of your mind helps you to accept and let go, allowing you to focus your energy on those things that you can change or influence.

CHAPTER 4

THE BALD, THE BEAUTIFUL AND LETTING GO OF YOUR BANANA

Be willing to let go of who you think you should be, in order to become who you are.

BRENÉ BROWN

Cancer is good at stripping away all of that you identify with yourself. Chemotherapy removes the superficial hair that many of us connect to our beauty, and the surgery occasionally requires amputation of the breast – which society associates with femininity. If a woman removes both breasts, loses her hair and perhaps even has her ovaries removed as well, is she not still a woman? Is she still not herself? The obvious answer would be yes to both of these questions. We obsess about the package we present to society, which most of the time is of little resemblance to who we are. To some extent, we don't remember who or what we are. When your superficial identity is stripped away, you have the opportunity to look in the mirror and say, 'Oh, I remember you.'

Finding yourself again

You can only be who you are. But who are you? The yogic practice of svadyaya is also part of Niyama or the second limb of yoga (along with tapas, discussed in the previous chapter). The word can be broken into svad, meaning the self, and dyaya, derived from dhyai and meaning to study, contemplate or think of. So svadyaya provides an invitation to pause, consider and reflect upon who you are. Our modern society, with its strong focus on social media culture, creates distraction from the 'self'. We seem to be a society obsessed with selfies, but we are outwardly creating images of what we desire others to see in us and concerned with projecting the perfect image. Our ego and pride are attached to what we believe we *should* look like and sound like. We no longer know what we want or like; instead, we want what others have just because they are a celebrity or an influencer. We have thoughts and beliefs that are not our own. We attach our identity to what we do, and our surface physical attributes.

I was once asked what it is like to be a female surgeon. I thought it an odd question and I could not answer it because I only know how it is to be a female surgeon – I have never experienced being a male surgeon. I can only imagine what it may be like to be something other than myself. The question is similar to being asked, 'How is it being a woman?' What comparison would there be? And really what does it matter?

In *A Return to Love*, author Marianne Williamson wrote,

> *Our deepest fear is not that we are inadequate. Our deepest fear is that we are powerful beyond measure. It is our light, not our darkness that most frightens us. We ask ourselves, who am I to be brilliant, gorgeous, talented, fabulous? Actually, who are you not to be?*

Yoga allows you to be yourself. It asks you to know yourself. With or without breasts, you are a woman. You are beautiful bald or with hair streaming down your back. You are beautiful. Because you can only be strong, beautiful, a woman. The essence of you is and will always be. You can only be who you are. Cancer, nor any other illness or treatment, cannot change who you are. You are constant. Your cancer has given you permission to be yourself. This doesn't mean you cannot or should not wear a wig, or make-up, or dress in beautiful clothing. I had a patient who had a very distinctive hairstyle that reminded me of a pirate's hat. She had three wigs made in an identical style to her original hairstyle – a red one, a blonde one and a brunette one. One day I looked at her and said, 'I think you are having way too much fun with the wigs.'

She turned, winked and said, 'You think?!'

Self-study versus fear

In some cultures, breast cancer is seen as being a result of 'karma'. Some believe that in a past life the woman has done something to deserve this illness in this lifetime. In those parts of the world, many women will not seek treatment and hide their suffering in shame. These women do not have the same options and choices as women in developed countries. Women in developed countries have treatment options because we have raised awareness of breast cancer and have developed screening programs to detect cancer at earlier stages.

Despite having more options and choices, many women still make a fear-based decision instead of an informed decision. Did you realise a woman who is a candidate to keep her breast and have a lumpectomy followed by radiation to the breast afterwards will, on average, live as long as a woman who has a mastectomy? But given the choice, and even after being told the survival is equivalent, many women still prefer to have a mastectomy.

Some cancers affect the leg – if I gave you the option to either have your leg amputated or keep your leg, which would you prefer? Similar to breast cancer, you could get a leg prosthetic and learn to run a marathon or ski with it, but I bet you would choose to keep your leg. You can live a perfectly good life without a leg as well as without a breast. And you would certainly not request the other leg to be removed if you had cancer in one leg! And yet, this is exactly what happens when cancer is found in one breast.

Fear can make us irrational. It is not wrong to have a mastectomy, but making a decision that is fear-based versus making an informed decision often creates unnecessary suffering and anxiety. Interestingly, studies have shown that women who live in regional and remote areas, even in developed countries, are more likely to be offered mastectomy and less likely to be offered reconstructive surgery. Ignorance creates confusion, while having information empowers you to decide – and ask for – what is right for you. When you know yourself well enough and have all available information, you can make the best, informed decision that you can live with. Confusion also feeds into doubt and we tend to second-guess what we should have done or not done, and so remaining attached to the past that cannot be changed.

Letting go of who you think you should be

When we hold on to anything too much, there is no space to receive something different and new. This reminds me of the story about catching a monkey. The story goes that, to catch a monkey in India, they take a coconut and make a hole in it just large enough for the monkey to place his hand inside. The coconut is tied to a tree. They place a banana inside the coconut. When the monkey finds the banana, he puts his hand inside and grabs hold of it. But when his hand is a clenched fist, it cannot fit back out through the hole and the monkey becomes trapped. The monkey can only free himself if he lets go of the banana. What are you holding onto that needs to be released?

I would not be the surgeon I am today if I held on tightly to the surgeon I thought I should be or was expected to be. My journey has been unconventional as a surgeon, but it has been so much more interesting and exciting because of it. I took risks in taking opportunities that were offered and made my share of mistakes. I made decisions that others questioned. If I had not let go of my image of what I thought a surgeon should be, I would not have become a yoga teacher while still practising surgery. I would not have integrated yoga and mindfulness into my surgical practice. Surgery and teaching yoga are what I do and reflections of who I am, but not who I am. It may seem strange to some, but I am not defined by others. We are complex, multidimensional beings and we are not our experiences. Therefore, you are not your cancer. It is only one of many experiences along your journey.

> **Yoga pose: Root to rise (urdhva hastasana)**
>
> From mountain (tadasana) pose, inhale and reach your arms overhead, keeping your shoulders away from the ears. Keep your sides long, feeling a stretch of your skin over the muscles and fibres along your side body.

> **Mindfulness exercise: Svadyaya**
>
> Svadyaya is the practice of self-inquiry and part of Niyama, the second limb of yoga, focusing on how we treat ourselves. What are the things that really bring you joy? Who do you love to spend time with and why? If you had only tomorrow, what matters most to you? If we really knew you, what would we know in particular about you?

Consider the breath as an example of letting go. After you take in an inhalation, you then must let the breath go, exhaling to receive the next breath of fresh air to nourish yourself. This is true of all things.

Finding support as you let go

The practice of ishvara pranidhana, the last part of Niyama (the second limb of yoga), is all about letting go and surrendering. As part of the practice, you recognise that you may experience discomfort, and could feel vulnerable, but you still allow yourself to let go while being supported. Ishvara means supreme or God, and pranidhana means to devote, dedicate or surrender. This reminds me of this popular saying, 'Let be, and let God'. This is not about whether you believe in God, or the universe, but is about understanding that there is something greater than ourselves.

As a surgeon, I am accustomed to finding solutions to help others with their struggles. And we all need the help of others at some point in time. Letting go of control while also allowing ourselves to be supported when we are vulnerable is part of experiencing the process.

I was reminded of the importance of allowing others to support me a few years ago, when I underwent a routine colonoscopy. I had so much abdominal pain before the procedure began, and after the procedure the pain worsened – so much so I was writhing on the bed of my Airbnb (I'd had to travel to the procedure) with my butt in the air, hoping to relieve myself. At one point, I asked to either have the pain go away or just die. Elizabeth, my friend and surgical colleague, was visiting me from Hawaii, and she called my doctor and drove me to the emergency room. I thought that this was actually normal, and maybe I was being weak and that possibly some of my patients had been through experiences like this and never complained.

When I got to the hospital, I then refused to let go of my surgeon hat, and tried to help the doctors figure out what was wrong with me. Instead of letting go of control and letting my colleagues do their job, I interfered by trying to stay in control. What resulted was a delay in the diagnosis of my bowel obstruction from a congenital adhesion. Even then I still did not want to give up control, and instead wanted to discuss the surgical approach and question every decision.

Doctors make the worst patients, but being a patient was good for me. I experienced things I had done for years to patients – for example, I had a nasogastric tube placed in my nose and down into my stomach, and the discomfort of it had tears running from my eyes.

In the end, my surgeon showed me my CT scan images. He said, 'Emilia, you know what needs to be done.' He was correct: I needed emergency surgery. I was feeling quite sorry for myself and my poor intestines. My surgeon was (and is) one of the best in the world. He even has instruments named after him. Nevertheless, a part of me called 'ego' still thought, *How can I help him to help me?* Of course, he didn't need my help. I eventually had to let go and trust the process.

I was fortunate to have my surgery completed laparoscopically using small incisions and a camera, but one of my port sites was painful for months. I had small bowel paralysis (called an 'ileus') afterwards and felt as if I had never exercised because my belly was bloated for a couple of weeks. I needed injections of blood-thinning medications in my belly to maintain blood flow to my intestines three times a day. I know this may sound strange, but I'm a surgeon who has a phobia of needles after a bad experience during childhood. I have never had difficulty giving needles to others, with compassion of course, but hate getting them myself.

However, I did what I was told I needed to do so I could recover. Letting go of control is not always easy, but the reality is I was never in control. It was an illusion. My body was in trouble and needed care. Even with my years of surgical knowledge and expertise treating this very condition, I still experienced fear and doubt that delayed and obstructed my care. When I stopped resisting and let go, I was able to receive the necessary treatment and heal.

Allowing myself to be present, I decided to experience the hospital fully. I discovered they had a wonderful selection of reading material, as well as movie channels. I watched *The Sound of Music*, which I had never seen to completion and which was excellent. I would stay up reading and watching movies, because I could sleep in and I had nowhere else to be. I made it like a retreat holiday at the Wesley Hospital. I enjoyed the tea cart, which would come around every afternoon, and the room service and meal selection (once I was able to eat again) was fabulous. I got to know the nurses and the staff. Although I would never want to have a bowel obstruction again, the experience gave me a different perspective, which I have appreciated.

Light and joy in discomfort?

Sometimes just trusting the process during our journey and being fully present during the experience, even during discomfort, helps. As my teacher Tammy Williams says, 'What if it isn't seen as a problem, but just as a strong passing sensation?' A woman experiencing childbirth, for example, has significant discomfort. She does so with the understanding that light and joy afterwards is coming afterwards. Many choose to endure it again with another pregnancy and birth. An experience such as illness also brings discomfort, during recovery and treatment. Could there be light and joy afterwards? Or during the process?

A person doesn't have the choice in having cancer; however, control does come in having a choice in the treatment of that cancer. You have the option of treatment and no treatment, or the option to choose particular treatments. Each choice creates an experience. Ishvara Pranidhana is more to do with letting go and being, rather than giving up. It is surrendering to that which is greater than ourselves. We could choose to just be and trust the treatments and the recovery process, observing how our body responds as if we are an impartial witness to the experience. We can choose to not have to do anything other than to just be with the experience, trusting that upon completion of the experience we move to the next experience, because nothing remains forever.

Yoga pose: Forward fold (uttanasana)

From root to rise (urdhva hastasana) pose, exhale and fold forward with a flat, elongated spine, reaching your fingertips towards your toes. Feel the stretch in the back body. If the stretch feels extreme or too intense, slightly bend your knees. Take a moment to notice whether your fingers reach the floor. What are your thoughts about what you have noticed? How does that thought make you feel? How does the feeling or emotion feel in the body itself?

Mindfulness exercise: Inhale to exhale

Hold your breath for as long as you can and then let it go and exhale. What does the feeling of letting go feel like? Can you recall a time when you did not want to give up control? How does being in control make you feel? How does feeling like you have to always be in control feel? What does it feel like when you can let go and know you will be supported? How does 'being' feel within the body? And how does this relate to your breath?

CHAPTER 5

THE GREAT STORYTELLER, YOUR MIND

*Do not judge me by my success; judge me by
how many times I fell down and got back up.*

NELSON MANDELA

I always thought of myself as a non-judgemental person until I attended a 'silent retreat'. When I was moving to Australia, I had wanted to do a silent retreat. I thought it would be a nice way to refresh my mindset as I began my transition. Many retreats had been filled with participants, and I couldn't decide which one to select. So one of my friends from Hawaii recommended a Vipassana 'retreat'. She said that the retreats were offered worldwide and were free to attend, including meals and accommodations. I thought this is incredible. Vipassana means insight or to see clearly the true nature of things. This also sounded pretty good.

So, as you do, I Googled Vipassana retreats and read the rules for attending. These included no stealing, no drugs, no sex and other basic things that would be quite easy to comply with and common sense.

I applied for a retreat offered in Australia five months in advance since these also fill up and have waiting lists. When the time came, I drove to a retreat centre six hours south of where I was living in Australia. It was a beautiful place. I checked in and they asked me to hand over my phone, car keys and any other valuables, which would be locked away until the end of the 10 days. I was provided with a map to my room and told there would be a daily schedule on the wall next to the bed in my room.

I walked through the beautiful grounds to my room and was shocked to see the schedule. Wake up at 4 am, meditation between 5 and 7 am, breakfast, more meditation from 9 to 11 am and lunch and then more meditation. I counted the hours of meditation and they added up to about ten hours out of the twelve-hour day. This was a meditation course not really a retreat. Oh, and did I mention that this was for ten days? There was to be ten days of no talking, not even any looking or gesturing to each other. No communication. There was also no reading, journalling, or exercising other than walking the grounds.

Judging in silence

One evening during a break between meditation sessions there was a long line at the restroom that extended outside. The air was fresh with a chill. I decided it made more sense to go inside and wait my turn because I was cold, so headed back in. Of course, it appeared as if I were cutting the long queue. A blonde lady in her twenties gave me a look. I could not tell her I was not cutting the queue and that I was just cold. So, I thought, *Great now she thinks I'm a selfish bitch*. So, since she didn't like me, I decided I didn't like her either. Over the following days, I avoided her.

Finally, the ninth day arrived, and we are allowed to speak at breakfast. I sat down with two other women I had met prior to the 'golden silence'. The blonde lady came and sat next to me. I thought, *Why is she sitting next to me when there are all of these other seats and tables available?* But then she looked at me with a big smile and said, 'Hello, I'm Olga. I've been wanting to meet you the entire time. I thought you were interesting.' I was shocked.

Dumbfounded, I introduced myself, and then quickly apologised for cutting the toilet queue. She had a confused look and said she didn't remember that. So, for the entire week I'd carried around this story about the blonde lady who thought I was a bitch for cutting the queue. I started to think I was a crazy woman who makes up stories about not only what I think of others, but also what they think of me. Completely idiotic. And then I realised I had judged everyone at the retreat. I'd made up stories about where I thought they were from, what their names were and what they did for a living. All completely wrong! Who does that? A crazy lady named Emilia. I remember wondering to myself how many other times I had made up stories in my mind about what others were thinking or even about myself.

More often than not, we have stories we tell ourselves. Initially, I did not recognise that I was judging the others at the retreat, but after several days of silence and increased awareness it was obvious how the mind creates stories to fill in any blanks. We do it instinctually to determine if our environment is safe. The place, person or thing in our environment is defined immediately and unconsciously, categorised and placed neatly into a box. This is a survival tactic to keep us safe, but we continue to use it even when we are in no danger.

Fear-based thinking (again)

Prior to attending the meditation course, my friends and colleagues joked with me to be careful, teasing it could be a cult and that they would convert me taking my money. I thought I'd dismissed the jokes and teasing, but something must have slipped in. On the fifth night I awoke startled. My bed and the floor of my room were shaking. I was afraid. I recalled what my friends had said about the course and it being a cult. My mind started to race. *Shit, what if they were right?* I thought

I remembered that the retreat staff had my car keys, my phone and all my valuables. I couldn't leave if I wanted to. It was dark outside. I started to imagine a story that could have come straight from a horror film. I scared myself even more with my imaginings. I could not sleep for what felt like hours.

Eventually, I drifted back to sleep. When I awoke the sun had risen and I had missed morning meditation as well as breakfast. When I emerged from my room, exhausted from lack of sleep, I saw two large kangaroos standing right outside. They stood about six feet tall with muscles and looked as if they had been lifting weights. They were eating the grass in front of my room. I realised it must have been the two of them through the night! They must have been under my cabin, which was raised from the ground. They had been bouncing around under my room during the night, making my floor and bed shake. My mind had created a fantastical story to explain the shaking of my bed, which resulted in fear and anxiety.

We have a tendency to look for evidence to support the story we have created in our heads. And the fear that comes from this is caused by false evidence appearing real (FEAR – that acronym I mentioned back in chapter 2). Of course, I could not share this with anyone as everyone was in silence. But I was relieved, amused and amazed – amazed because I became aware that my assessment of the situation was incorrect. I had misjudged the entire event and created an elaborate story to justify this judgement. What else had I misjudged in my past? What other stories had I told myself? But gaining more awareness of the mind's tendency to create stories can help us to reduce misjudgement of our environment, each other and, most importantly, ourselves. We can really take time to ponder is this thought or story real?

Comparison and judgement

Comparison can also manifest as judgement. Perhaps another breast cancer patient tells you of their journey through treatment and assures you that your journey most likely will be just as terrible. What happens if it is not? Perhaps they do not want to associate with you anymore. The source of these actions is judgement.

When my sister had breast cancer, she attended a support group. She was made to feel unwelcome, however, because her breast cancer was an early-stage cancer not requiring chemotherapy. Since she did not require chemotherapy or have stage 4 cancer, some people in the group felt that she could not possibly understand what they had experienced. This is what I call 'breast cancer shaming'.

You can still have empathy without having the same experience as another. The reality is each of us has our own unique experience anyway. Our experiences may appear to have similarities, but as individuals it is impossible to have the exact same experience. Fear is fear, whether you are stage 1 or 4. The physiologic aspects of fear and how it arises within the body and the breath is the same. Pupils dilate, and your blood pressure and heart rate increase. These are measurable physiologic changes, regardless of the root of your fear. Do not tell me that it differs if you are this stage of cancer or that stage. Do not allow someone else to put you inside a small categorical box of judgement. You are large and expansive and do not fit inside of any category. You are not a stage 1 or a stage 4. You are not a triple negative cancer or a BRCA positive or negative person. Those are classifications of cancer or genetic risk, but they are not the person. Remember who you are. Recall your greatness and the essence of who you are. Cancer cannot change your fundamental being, unless you allow it.

We often tend to judge ourselves more harshly than others. And we then confuse our thoughts as beliefs. Another patient of mine, let's call her Christine, had undergone bilateral mastectomies and reconstruction using her tissue to replace her breast. This is called autologous reconstruction. She was still four years from completion of her treatment, but presented every few months with concerns of new lumps, believing her cancer had returned. Because of these fears, she had extensive workup looking for cancer. Neither a physical exam nor imaging would find anything.

Christine was seeing a psychiatrist to help her mental state of excessive worrying about the cancer. She was still convinced her cancer had returned, and had difficulty believing she could be cured of cancer. She once said if anything bad was going to happen, it would happen to her. She believed that if there was a 1 per cent chance of a particular complication, she would have that too. Despite the evidence being otherwise, she continued to have these negative thoughts.

I asked her how she would feel if 40 years had passed and she was still worrying about the cancer returning, even though it never had. She would have wasted her life worrying. As Jon Kabat-Zinn said, 'He who dies before he dies, does not die when he dies.'

Yoga pose: Halfway lift (ardha uttanasana)

From your forward fold (uttanasana) fill your lungs and lift to a flat back with your hands on your shins or fingertips to the floor. Chin is slightly tucked to maintain the line from the tailbone through the crown of your head. Exhale and as you release your breath, let go again, folding forward and extending hands towards your mat.

Mindfulness exercise: Listing common thoughts

Write a list of common thoughts that often come to mind. On a scale of 1 to 10, how often do you think of each thought? Write this number next to the thought. Then write for each whether it is a true statement. Do you really believe it of yourself or is it a story that your mind has created?

Recognising vulnerability, without judgement

In surgery, we audit ourselves and our peers with morbidity and mortality reviews. While I was in surgical training, we would stand in front of the entire department to discuss our mistakes and explain the rationale behind our decisions of what we did during an operation. The intention was to learn from each other and to improve surgical outcomes. And this process does achieve this outcome if undertaken with mutual respect and lack of judgement. However, this was not always the case. No matter how good you are, a surgeon will eventually have a complication. If a surgeon says they never have a complication, either they are not being honest, or they have not operated enough. It is a tremendous responsibility to be trusted with another's life and not to be taken lightly.

Many years ago, I was removing a gallbladder from a staff member of the hospital. She chose me as her surgeon, because she trusted me and believed I was very capable. She had seen me operate before and respected my surgical skills. The day I was performing her surgery, I was notified my mother had died. I knew this day would come. I felt calm and knew I just needed to complete the day and then I would arrange to fly from Hawaii where I was living at the time to Oklahoma to my mother's home. The case was simple and straightforward. I had done it hundreds of times. I even got a cholangiogram, which is an X-ray of the bile ducts, although it was not necessary. The dye went into the small bowel, which was normal.

Once the surgery was complete, I left for three weeks to handle my mother's and my family's affairs. When I returned, my best friend and colleague told me that my patient had been transferred to another hospital because I had cut the common bile duct. I thought she was joking. She said, 'I didn't want to tell you, because you were away at your mother's funeral'. *No, no, no ... this is impossible*, I thought. I went over the surgery in my head many times, to determine how I could have made this error – the most serious complication of gallbladder surgery. I felt terrible and really questioned my abilities. Interestingly, I had never had this complication before after performing hundreds of gallbladder removals and now, after having it once, I was questioning my abilities and dismissing the other successful surgeries I had performed over the previous ten years. Fortunately, my patient recovered from the complication, although another operation was required to repair her duct.

She returned to my clinic and told me that her friends said that she should sue me, but she told me that she knew I did not intentionally harm her. She did not sue me, but the story did not end there. When her sister needed her gallbladder removed, she came to my clinic for consultation. Pretty quickly, I asked why she came to me and not another surgeon. She looked at me and said, simply, 'You are our family's surgeon.' They believed in me more than I believed in myself. I completed the surgery, removing her gallbladder successfully.

At that moment, when I was feeling low and doubting myself, I had negative thoughts about my abilities, which were not true. I am a good surgeon, but I do make mistakes as all surgeons do and have. I did not recognise my vulnerability at the time of my mother's passing and that I should have asked for help during my cases.

We tend to believe and have been taught that vulnerability is weakness. However, asking for help and learning from failure – or in this case a serious surgical complication – take strength. Having occasional thoughts of inadequacy, doubt and feeling as though you are not enough is not uncommon – as research professor Brené Brown explains in *Daring Greatly*, being in the 'arena' means that 'uncertainty, risk and emotional exposure are not optional'. Our unwillingness to feel vulnerable, our desire to protect ourselves from discomfort, and our disengagement are all a reflection and measure of our fear.

The stories we tell ourselves to avoid further pain or suffering are not always accurate. The only way I could avoid another gallbladder surgery complication was to stop doing gallbladder surgery. For that matter, the way for me to avoid all surgical complications would be to quit surgery altogether. Cultivating a mindset of non-judgement is not only about judgement of others, but judgement of ourselves. The awareness that you are not your thoughts allows you to act upon that knowledge. It gives you the opportunity to take a breath in. It gives you permission to forgive yourself and others. Regardless of your circumstances and struggles, you are strong and have the capacity to overcome. You have an amazing capacity to heal and restore, despite mental and physical vulnerability. The body and mind are resilient. You are resilient.

Yoga pose: Lunge (anjaneyasana)

From your forward fold (uttanasana), reach your right foot back as far as it will go and lunge with the left knee forward. You can keep your hands framing your left foot, or reach them upwards towards the sky. Inhale in as you find length in your spine, reaching the crown of your head upwards (or forwards if hands are still on the floor). If hands are reaching upwards, sweep the arms overhead while opening your chest.

Mindfulness exercise: Listing your strengths

Write a list of your strengths. Then write a list of those qualities you (or others) would commonly call your weaknesses or faults. (I prefer to call these qualities that do not serve our higher self.) Consider which list is longer. Which list was easier to compose?

CHAPTER 6

UNLOCKING THE SECRET MYSTERIES OF THE UNIVERSE INSIDE

Patience is not our ability to wait, but the ability to keep a good attitude while waiting.

JOYCE MEYER

After surgery, perhaps you started chemotherapy. If so, no doubt you were disappointed that it was going to take months to complete. You just wanted to 'get this whole thing over with'. When I meet with my patients, this is exactly what many say: 'Let's just get on with it. I want this thing out of me.' Perhaps you received 'AC' every three weeks and then 'T' every week for 12 weeks. Perhaps you made a friend who had the same regimen and treatment days. You looked forward to chatting with her and, now that treatment has finished, you still meet up for the occasional coffee. During those months of treatment, you read a few books and caught up on your Netflix. No doubt you are usually too busy to read and had not taken the time for a good book in a couple of years. Maybe chemotherapy gave you an opportunity to sit in the recliner chair, put your feet up, have a conversation with a stranger (now your friend) and read a book. Perhaps you'd had that desire for a while now. You'd said to your husband you wished you could slow down. Well, during your treatment you got a regularly scheduled appointment with a recliner chair, a good book and good conversation with lovely people – scheduled for every three weeks and weekly thereafter for a few months.

Looking for opportunities in delays

Dealing with delays and having to wait forces us to slow down, usually much to our frustration. Instead of being frustrated, however, try to look for the opportunity in the delay. It is not often that we choose to be still. My friend Kerri wrote *Do Talk to Strangers*, a book that highlights everyone has a story. You have a story as well. Of all the people we meet, how many do we take the time to really get to know? The friends you made from chemotherapy, would you have met them otherwise? And if you had, would you have really taken the time to get to know them? And no doubt you found you had more in common than breast cancer.

Patience is a quality that I knew I needed to work on during my early twenties. One of the personality characteristics of surgeons is decisiveness and fulfilment from the immediate gratification of seeing the results from an operation. We don't ponder for long periods of time as to whether a medicine will work or not, or whether we should operate or not. We usually make those decisions quickly. Sitting and watching a patient, and not operating, is much more difficult. Having the patience to determine if a patient will improve with conservative management or get worse is challenging.

I'm sure you also had moments of stillness on the days after your chemotherapy. You knew that you would not feel completely yourself. You had this awareness and started to know how you would respond to the chemotherapy, so you learned what to do to support yourself during those times. You could feel the arising of nausea and could manage. But chemotherapy is done now. Do you still have an awareness of that which is arising within?

Mastering external influences

The practice of Pratyahara, the fifth limb of yoga, involves the withdrawal of the senses, or turning off the senses to external influences. It is one of the most difficult and sometimes challenging aspects of yoga to understand. Our senses are filters that we use to define, experience and give context to our environment. Thinking of it in these terms may help you understand it further: withdrawing our sense means not being distracted by the constant internal chatter from our busy minds, which swings from one thought to the next, or by the external stimulation from the outside world. So many smells, sounds and visual stimulation can distract us, as well as provide us with experiences.

The ability to look inwards and understand what is inside of ourselves, without the distraction of external stimuli or the internal negative chatter of worry, fear and planning is important. What is happening on the inside? Most of our experiences with our environment come from at least one of our five senses. How does this or that taste or smell? What are the qualities of sounds in the ear or sights that are pleasing? The practice of Pratyahara allows you to awaken to a world within, and this can be very interesting. You can unearth that part of yourself that is quiet and waiting to be discovered and not defined by the experiences of the senses interacting with external stimuli.

Once a patient told me that she knew something was not right within herself. Occasionally I have patients come to me saying the same. For many, the feeling comes from anxiety and often they have nothing wrong with them. But I knew this patient was quite level headed. In contrast to Christine (who I mention in the previous chapter), whose doubt was arising from fear, this patient's concern was arising from a deeper self-awareness. She said that she could not tell me exactly what was wrong, but she knew her cancer had returned. I scanned her and examined her and found nothing. She also had a subtle area that was firm at her reconstruction site and I biopsied the area. The pathology was benign. I continued to follow her closely and, after a few months, saw the area was still present. I did another MRI. Gotcha! A small mass that could now be seen and biopsied under image guidance. This time the cancer recurrence was confirmed. She was treated for the recurrence and is alive and well today.

In contrast, John was referred to me for consultation regarding breast cancer risk and genetic testing. John's mother had died from breast cancer and, at the time of first seeing me, his 27-year-old daughter was being treated for a triple negative breast cancer and had tested positive for the breast cancer gene (BRCA). John told me that he didn't believe he was at risk because he was a man, but that his daughter had insisted he get checked just in case. Although breast cancer is more common in women, 1 per cent of breast cancer occurs in men. I have treated men with breast cancer in my practice, and perform genetic testing on anyone I see who is at risk.

During the physical examination, I noticed that John had some mild breast enlargement. This can occur in ageing men (called gynecomastia or, in layman's terms, 'man boobs'). But in his left breast I felt a small lump. I ordered a mammogram and biopsy. Yes, John also had breast cancer that we successfully treated surgically and he too tested positive for the BRCA breast cancer gene. Most likely his breast cancer had been there for years. We don't speak much about male breast cancer and nor do we emphasise the practice of personal breast examinations in men. But, regardless of whether we are male or female, we must learn to practice self-awareness of our whole being.

At times, someone can be very in tune with themselves. They internally know what is happening even when this can't be confirmed with a test or an obvious external sign. Of course, I am saying this with caution because I don't want you to worry that every little pain or feeling is a sign of cancer or recurrence. On the contrary – you don't want to live in unnecessary fear and worry. But you can develop a practice of inner knowingness and awareness of any internal shifts. You can be in tune with yourself to know when your body and your mind require support, and access this support before they break down.

It goes without saying that practising Pratyahara may not diagnose a cancer or prevent a cancer. It can, however, awaken an awareness of what is happening inside through an inward focus and paying attention with intention. Having an experience with the outside world and using our senses to appreciate those experiences is not wrong, but we live most of our life in the external world without ever experiencing that which is within. Being still and taking a moment to look within without distraction can be a gift and beneficial.

Yoga pose: High plank (kumbhakasana)

From your lunge (anjaneyasana) pose, place both hands on the floor beside your left foot (if they are not there already). With palms flat on the mat, step your left foot back, placing your hands shoulder-width apart on the mat while lowering your hips into a plank.

The joints are stacked with the wrists beneath the elbows and shoulders. Extend your tailbone towards the heels as you engage your core, navel to spine. Find length in your side waists. The knees can be up or down on the mat. Inhale as you widen your collar bones, allowing your shoulder blades to come towards each other.

As you hold your plank for a few breaths, explore your attitude or quality of mind when you are physically challenged or experiencing discomfort. Can you find stillness and ease? Can you be patient while having the experience?

Mindfulness exercise: Withdrawing from your senses

To have a better understanding of how engaged you are with the outside world, try withdrawing from your senses for 10 minutes. Turn off the TV, radio and computer. Switch off the notifications from your smartphone, Facebook, Twitter, emails and so on. Go into a very quiet place where you feel safe and where there are no obvious smells or visual distractions.

Once you have removed or decreased external distractions, try closing your eyes and decreasing the internal distractions. We use our senses to define images within our minds. Decreasing the noise within the mind and reining in our thoughts may be the most difficult.

Try to sit in stillness and silence for one minute without doing anything or responding to anything that arises. Continue to practise this exercise, extending the amount of time each day or every few days. Afterwards, write down how you feel, your thoughts and what you have discovered about yourself.

CHAPTER 7

TICK-TOCK ON THE CLOCK, THE TIME FOR JOY IS NOW

Perfection in an asana is achieved when the effort to perform it becomes effortless.

PATAÑJALI

When you were going through chemotherapy, you sometimes likely felt nauseated or sick. And chances are your goal was just getting through it all and delaying joy until it was over. Then perhaps you decide to delay feeling joy until you reach two years without a recurrence. And once you reach that goal? You decide to delay joy until you reach five years survival. And that is exactly what could happen, and what it means is that you are continuing to delay your joy and you are not truly living – you are just surviving. Is it possible to be content and joyful now despite the challenge?

Striving for happiness or acceptance and contentment?

We have all had moments of thinking that if only we had this, could do that or things were like this, then we would be happy. *If only* ... I too have been in that place of thinking if only I had more money or could complete this goal, then I would be fine. Happiness and contentment (or satisfaction), however, are two distinctly different things.

Dr Daniel Kahneman, a psychologist, economist and Nobel laureate, studied happiness and observed that many people were not actually seeking happiness, but long-term satisfaction. Kahneman argues, once we have enough money to meet our basic needs such as food, clothing and shelter, our happiness plateaued. Wealth beyond that needed to meet our basic needs does not increase happiness. Happiness is dependent on circumstances or on certain conditions being present. Contentment or satisfaction, on the other hand, could be found regardless of the circumstances or conditions we find ourselves in. This concept is related to the practice of santosa, part of Niyama (the second limb of yoga). Santosa is all about practising contentment, accepting what has happened and choosing joy despite it all.

A few years ago I saw a living example of this. While I was in high school, a close family friend was diagnosed with breast cancer. She worked with my mother as a teacher and was like a second mother to me. Her daughter was like a sister. So we were close! I remember she had a mastectomy and chemotherapy. We were young so I didn't know all the details of her cancer journey, but I was aware that over many years she had various treatments. She is now 80 years old, and a few years ago, when returning home to California, I visited with her. I reflected on her many years and that, despite her cancer and the treatments, she had continued to live a full life. She had remarried to a jazz musician, moved into a beautiful home, watched her children get married and have grandchildren, and is still friends with her ex-husband.

She made a choice to be happy despite her struggles and sometimes physical sufferings.

These days, many are striving to acquire material things or career titles to achieve the picture of how society defines success. Striving originates from a mindset that there is scarcity or lack. Similarly, stealing arises from a feeling of scarcity or lack from not having or being enough. The desire for more arises from within to fill a void. We look outside of ourselves to what others seem to have that we don't have, or to what others seem to be that we are not.

Stealing can involve more than material objects

Yama, the first limb of yoga, is similar to the second limb, Niyama, in that it has further practices within it. Part of Yama is the practice of asteya, or non-stealing. You may not literally steal material things, but stealing can manifest in other ways. Let's look at another example.

Barbara was an executive at a large American bank. Her mother and sister had both had breast cancer. Despite the significant family history of breast cancer, when Barbara developed a lump in her breast, instead of immediately seeking medical attention, she did nothing. When she finally came in to see me and disrobed for me to examine her breast cancer during our first meeting, what I found was a large fungating mass (that is, it had become like a fungus in appearance) coming out of the skin which bled. I was shocked. This was the kind of mass you would see in a developing country, not in a metropolitan teaching hospital in the US. How could an intelligent, high-powered businesswoman allow this to happen?

She looked into my disapproving eyes. (At that time in my career, I had not yet mastered my poker face.) Before I could say anything, she said, 'I knew it was cancer, but I am an executive and have my career to consider.' At this point, what was there to say? What was done, was done. She was rising in the ranks of the bank and soon after became a vice-president. She desires to have this title and position so much that she robbed herself of her health.

To treat her cancer, she required chemotherapy, radiation and aggressive surgical intervention with removal of her breast and advanced plastic surgery techniques just to close the wound. Her treatments and recovery took many months and years. The ripple effect was time away from work and family. She robbed others of their time as well. The bank had to provide long-term coverage for her absence. All this could have potentially been avoided through earlier detection or at least intervention at the time she had first noticed the lump. Caring for yourself and loving yourself is a great manifestation of our love for others.

Setting goals and having a plan of the steps we need to take in our careers and overall lives are fine, but Barbara assumed that if she took time out to care for herself, she would not advance in her career. The overall goal is still achievable but possibly the timing and path may be different than planned. If we are attached to the outcome and how the journey should be, we may create more struggle and suffering.

Yoga pose: Low plank (chaturanga dandasana)

As you exhale in high plank (kumbhakasana), hug the elbows in towards the body and lower your body, with control, towards your mat, while maintaining the straight line from the tailbone to the crown of your head. If necessary, put your knees down to maintain the integrity of the pose.

> **Mindfulness exercise: Items you desired and acquired**
>
> Write a list of all the things that in the past you desired. Also write down those that you acquired. If you own a car, you are already in the top 1 per cent in the world!
>
> Now write a list of all that you have accomplished, starting with the obvious things (for example, maybe you have graduated from school, you are a parent, or you have achieved a particular goal that you had set for yourself). Next, extend the list to include even the smallest of things (for example, finding time for a walk or a movie). Next, how did it make you feel to acquire or achieve? How do you feel about those same things now?

Finding neutrality

A healthy lady referred to me for breast cancer, let's call her Jocelyn, was angry because she felt she had done everything 'right'. She had followed a very strict diet, exercised daily, maintained her ideal body weight and had no family history of breast cancer – and yet here she was with this disease. She asked me why she had breast cancer. I turned the question back on her and asked her why she thought she had developed breast cancer. I didn't know why she developed breast cancer and, at times, can never identify a singular cause.

The moment she walked into the room, I could feel Jocelyn's heightened, almost frantic and uncontrolled, energy. 'Why couldn't someone else have my breast cancer?' she asked.

I responded by asking, 'Who else would you prefer to have it? You wouldn't want your mother or sister to have it, would you?'

'Well, of course I wouldn't,' she said. 'But I'm so angry because I do everything right. And now this!'

'If you knew you would end up with breast cancer, would you have eaten crappy food, got fat and smoked?' I asked. 'If you'd done so, you would have felt like crap and have other health problems. You have done the best that you could to prevent illness, but the reality is that illness is part of the human experience. You have probably experienced the flu despite doing everything right. Correct?' She told me that wasn't the same thing, but I told her you can also die from the flu. Wanting to move on to the positives, I said, 'You got your screening mammogram. You are in the best shape for treatment, more than most patients. You have an early cancer that can be treated.'

After her treatments were completed, during her follow-up visits we began discussing how she had benefited from living a healthy lifestyle, despite her developing breast cancer. Breast cancer has many risk factors and the cause is not always easily determined. Even if you have a healthy lifestyle, you have no guarantees that you will never be ill. We live a healthy lifestyle so that we can enjoy living in the moment much more. However, physical challenges are part of being human.

Aparigraha, also part of Yama (the first limb of yoga), is the practice of non-attachment or neutrality to the outcome of our actions. Being attached to outcome, instead of just being present and experiencing our actions without judgement, causes suffering. Recall the Law of Impermanence discussed in chapter 3, and that all things are on a continuum of change, including ourselves. Aparigraha is about developing equanimity, a state of calm composure, undisturbed by phenomena. It means to be unshaken by or neutral to that which is positive or negative. It is not being unfeeling or unemotional, but is a quality of mind that is neutral with acceptance. This quality of mind allows you to deal with whatever the outcome. You can have a 'clear' mind to decide how to respond to any situation you are in.

Mindfulness exercise: Being neutral

Many women who have experienced breast cancer experience anxiety when they go for an annual mammogram or other testing that looks for a possible recurrence or a new cancer. This anxiety or fear creates stress, until the results return that all is well.

Is it possible for you to practise being neutral in this situation? Your anxiety or fear will not alter the outcome. Allow yourself to accept whatever the result and then create space to respond appropriately to those results the best that you can. This may be very difficult, and is easier said than done. The next time that you go for testing of any kind, however, can you be neutral and not attached to the outcome?

CHAPTER 8

THE SOUTHERN HEMISPHERE: CYCLONES, MUD AND VAGINAS

No mud, no lotus.

THICH NHAT HANH

I recently had a patient ask me about using cannabis oil in breast cancer treatment. I hadn't heard of this. Occasionally, I have patients inquire about other possible breast cancer treatments. When I met a patient I'll call Nicole, she was 36 and had a large tumour in her breast which she wanted to treat with an alternative medical treatment that involved the infusion of vitamins. I never tell patients that something won't work, because one thing I know for sure is when someone strongly believes something they just believe it. Also, I do not know everything and maybe there is something out in the world that I have not heard of that may work.

So I asked Nicole how successful the treatment would be, but she didn't know. I went on to explain that I could tell her the success rate and survival rates of surgery, chemotherapy and radiation, stage for stage. Often, I wonder how a person decides to trust information that they receive and determine its credibility. I encouraged her to ask the guy who was going to treat her more questions, and to request that he provide his success rates with this treatment. We also agreed to try it her way as an experiment for a short while. She agreed to have her MRI, which does not require radiation and I needed to do anyway for treatment planning. She would do her infusions for only one month. Then we would reimage her to see what progress she had made. If the tumour had decreased in size, then great – we would keep going. If not, then she agreed that she would try what I was recommending.

When Nicole returned after a month, the tumour was slightly larger. Although disappointed (as despite our previous agreement), she still did not agree to having chemotherapy. She had four small children and questionable partner. But then she returned a few days later, saying her partner had given her an ultimatum to do chemotherapy or he would leave her. This was not coming from concern of her wellbeing, mind you, but because he didn't want to take care of their children. I could not tell her what I really thought of him, because what I thought was, *Good riddance, let him take a walk. You don't need someone like him, who is not supportive.* I knew she needed the best mindset possible during treatment to optimise healing. Worrying and additional stress beyond her cancer diagnosis would create a physiological environment not conducive to recovery.

The ultimatum did mean she completed the neoadjuvant chemotherapy (chemotherapy before surgery) and the tumour reduced in size so much so that we were able to perform a lumpectomy, removing all the cancer within the breast, while simultaneously lifting and reconfiguring the breast so it looked even better than before the procedure. This is called oncoplastic surgery. We also did the other breast for symmetry. We would joke that we had to lift the other breast, because otherwise it would get jealous that it didn't get cancer and look as good. Nicole had a great sense of humour.

Growing from the struggle and challenge

'No mud, no lotus' is one of my favourite quotes. A lotus flower only grows from mud. Something so beautiful arises from something considered disgusting. Similarly, during times of struggle and challenge we grow the most. We learn valuable lessons and can become stronger. During our most trying times, we must trust the process and the journey, and that all will be well.

The storm will end. Have you ever been through a hurricane (as they're known in the Northern Hemisphere) or cyclone (Southern Hemisphere)? It is crazy and chaotic and, when it ends, there is a quiet calm. In the calm, you can take account of the damage done. All that could not withstand the storm will have been washed away and this provides a cleansing. You can start to rebuild, better and stronger than before, to withstand the next storm. Because you know another storm will one day come. Illness is like a storm. It washes away bad habits, relationships and stressful jobs.

Perhaps you're wondering what happened to Nicole's partner? He was too weak to stick around. He got washed out to sea by the cyclone. He was on his own journey and needed to move on. Trusting that life will be even better afterwards starts with trusting yourself. And trust arises from honesty. Satya is the value of honesty and part of Niyama, the second limb of yoga. Satya is not just about honesty with others but, most importantly, honesty with ourselves and how we treat ourselves.

Finding and speaking your truth

Despite her partner leaving her during her treatment, Nicole remained upbeat and positive. She was always happy and teased me when she came for her surveillance visits. She would laugh and say, 'Are you taking photos of my great-looking boobs?' (I would take photos to place in her medical record to document the healing process.)

When her cancer recurred, she decided not to have further treatment. Her team of doctors and support staff asked if she required assistance for her children and whether she had her affairs in order. She had assured us she had taken care of everything. When Nicole died, she had no will and her family did not know her cancer had returned. She was not truthful with others and possibly with herself. Of course, Nicole was only in her thirties, and most at that age are not considering their affairs. The reality is, regardless of age or whether we have a life-threatening illness, we should have our affairs in order. Satya is not just speaking the truth, but also seeing the truth. There is freedom in the truth. It can be a heavy burden to carry secrets. Satya requires us to trust ourselves and then to trust others. Withholding the truth is a form of lying and we do it because we do not trust the response to the truth. Everything done in the dark eventually comes into the light.

Yoga pose: Cobra (bhujangasana)

From low plank (chaturanga dandasana), lower yourself completely to your mat. As you inhale, place your hands next to your chest and extend your spine backwards, widening the collar bones, while opening your chest and heart. Keep your hips and thighs on your mat.

What arises in the body when your heart is open? What happens with your breath when you are open?

Mindfulness exercise: Uncovering secrets and lies

Write down a secret that you have kept in the past or are currently holding. How did/does it make you feel to keep it? How does the fear of it being discovered feel? How did it feel when it came to light? If it hasn't, explore what it might feel like when it does.

Clearing a new path

In contrast, another patient, let's call her Corrine, was a married mother of two school-aged children with a supportive husband, Larry. She was an active athlete, as an outrigger canoe paddler. The rest of the family was also into competitive water sports. Corrine was diagnosed at age 34 and required a mastectomy. Because of her young age, she chose bilateral mastectomy for risk reduction. The breast imaging underestimated the size of her tumour and she required post-mastectomy radiation after undergoing immediate reconstruction. She sailed through her surgery, but the chemotherapy took its toll.

After recovering, she had the required radiation. Through it all, Larry and her children were there for her, including during some very challenging days that were spent in the emergency department and the occasional hospitalisation. With the support of her husband and family, the children still made it to school and athletic events. When Christmas came around, she asked her children, 'Do you want to go to Fiji for Christmas as a family, which means no presents but being able to make memories together? Or we can stay home, and you will get presents like every other year?' Her young children chose making memories together. So, instead of accumulating more stuff, they decided as a family that creating memories was a priority – something that they had not considered before. Her cancer not only affected her perspective, but also that of her husband and children.

The cyclone not only clears away that which is no longer best for you, making space for something better, but also clears a way so you can see clearly that which is strong and long-lasting.

Whether you are Christian or not, you've likely heard of the story of Jesus healing a man born blind. As described in John 9:1-12, Jesus used mud and covered the man's eyes before the mud is washed clean and he could see. Something that is considered dirty and opaque was used to clear vision, but in the story the blind man had to walk to clean water first to wash the mud away from his eyes. It was through trust and faith that he could see eventually clearly, with renewed sight and perspective.

> **Mindfulness exercise: Finding trust**
>
> Recall times when you experienced challenges in your life, whether with your cancer, or during financial loss, divorce or any other struggle. Who were those who supported and lifted you? Who did you trust? Close your eyes and notice as you recall having experienced full trust in yourself and someone. How does it feel or manifest in your body as sensations of trusting and being trusted? How does it manifest in your breath?

The other southern hemisphere

Let me ask: how are things in the southern hemisphere? I mean, how are things downtown? Yes, I am talking about your vagina. After getting to know my patients well, by the second year of their surveillance the formerly happy patient often breaks into tears. When I ask what was happening, they say, 'Oh, it's nothing'.

'But it is something,' I say. 'Because you are usually smiling and joking with me, but today you are tearful.' She then goes on to tell me she doesn't enjoy 'it' anymore.

'Enjoy what?' I ask.

'Sex … It is painful. I've tried lubricants, but I just don't feel good about myself.'

If this is how you're feeling, you are not alone. Trying to understand if this is a result of treatment and something new, or if some pre-existing elements are involved is difficult. I have had to learn to determine the 'sexual baseline' prior to treatment and have an honest discussion with the patient, and sometimes the patient's partner, as to how treatment could impact sexual health. We discuss options for addressing side effects of treatment, such as laser, radiofrequency, and even platelet-rich plasma treatments for vaginal rejuvenation, because some breast cancer treatments can cause premature menopause. Unlike when prescribing for natural menopause, we cannot place many who have had breast cancer on estrogen supplementation because of its increased risk of causing recurrence.

Finding alternative, safe methods to improve sexual health after cancer treatment is a growing area of interest. Occasionally, referral to a sexual therapist to provide counselling for the mental aspects of sexual dysfunction is required. But I do know that maintaining healthy intimate connections with your partner positively affects your mental, as well as your physical, wellbeing. Our relationships are affected by challenges and struggle. How we manage or respond during times of suffering will affect those we share our lives with, at home and at work. Many who experience breast cancer will have a lack of sexual energy and desire, but healthy intimate connections are important to our health. In my earlier years as a surgeon, I hadn't realised that many women silently suffer and have relationship problems as a result.

Brahmacharya is another practice within Yama, the first limb in yoga. The practice translates as adopting a behaviour that leads us to the divine. It is often associated with celibacy, which is usually not a problem for women undergoing breast cancer treatment. It is so much more than that, however; it is, more broadly, the correct use of our energy, including sexual energy. So although it's great to help you get your 'sexy back', you can use other ways to reconnect and have emotional intimacy, without relying on the physical component (which should not be overlooked or diminished).

In more recent times, people all over the world are craving connection. We look externally or to social media to connect. Before you connect with another, you must first connect to yourself. It can be uncomfortable to be alone with yourself; however, I say disconnect to connect. In the introduction, I mention the saying that 'wherever you go, that's where you are'. At the end of the day, when your eyes are closed in darkness, you are left with yourself. Do you like being with yourself? Is connecting with yourself uncomfortable? Are you comfortable in the company of you? If you don't want to spend time with you, who will?

And to learn more about options for sexual challenges after breast cancer, visit my website at www.personalrenewal.com.au.

> ### Mindfulness exercise: Booking in a time out
>
> Let your family and friends know that you are choosing to spend some time with yourself and that you will not be reachable by phone or any other device, so they do not worry. Recall a time when you spent quality time (if ever) with yourself doing what you desired for yourself and not following the desires of others.
>
> Spend a minimum of two hours spending time with yourself, and do not check your device during that time. You may feel lost without a device, but until quite recently we did not have mobile phones or other devices, and the world did not end and children survived.
>
> In this time, do something that you enjoy doing that you normally would not do alone – but this time, go only with yourself. Maybe take yourself to a movie or an outdoor activity. Afterwards, spend time writing down how you felt spending quality time with yourself and doing something that you chose to do. How did that feel? Was it difficult or easy? Did you enjoy the time or feel lost without someone with you? Were there feelings of guilt or selfishness? Were there feelings of stress that you were not getting things done that needed to be completed?

CHAPTER 9

YOUR MINDSET, YOUR HEALTH, YOUR RESPONSIBILITY

Change the way you look at things and the things you look at change.

WAYNE DYER

Your perspective is everything. A few years after completing my surgical oncology training, I was working at a tertiary hospital in the Pacific Northwest. An eighty-six-year-old gentleman from Montana was referred to me. He was a runner and ran six miles per day (more than I was running), but was complaining of swelling in his legs that was preventing him from running as far. The CT scan showed a tumour compressing the inferior vena cava (the largest vein in the body in the abdomen), but it appeared it could be removed. I had seen during my vascular surgery rotation that the vena cava could be reconstructed from a leg vein using what's called a spiral graft. I had never done this operation (removing the vena cava) and nor had I seen it done for a tumour. But I planned this as a backup and had a vascular surgeon available to help if I needed.

The tumour was a sarcoma. Sarcomas are tricky because their appearance on imaging may not be how they appear in surgery. This sarcoma was arising from the inferior vena cava, but firmly stuck to the aorta (the largest artery in the body). Basically, we need both large blood vessels. They carry a large amount of blood throughout the body. I was assisted by one of the chief residents. I worked for a couple of hours trying to dissect the tumour away from the aorta. It was slowly coming apart, but I began to doubt whether it was possible to remove it.

The chief resident kept saying it was impossible and we should give up. The anaesthetist asked me what I was going to do because time was passing and he preferred to not keep someone of his age under anaesthesia for too long. Too much input from the peanut gallery. I thought, *Shut up so I can think.*

If I did not remove the tumour, he would die. If I proceeded and caused significant bleeding, he could die in the operating room or from complications afterwards. I felt heavy. I decided to take a short break from operating and went to the toilet. The toilet is a quiet place, and I could think and pray. I did my business and prayed. I remember saying to God, 'Please give me the wisdom to stop and not harm him if that is the right thing to do. But if the tumour can be removed, please show me how.' As I said, parts of this required operation were new to me. (After all, it is impossible to learn and encounter every situation in surgical training.) But I did feel a little calmer after my toilet visit.

A new perspective

I returned to the operating room, and decided to stand on the opposite side of the operating table. I started my dissecting and it was again slowly coming away from the aorta. I stopped and noticed what I had not before. My patient had several collateral vessels (new blood vessels that the body forms because of obstruction) that were already providing blood flow. Since the tumour was already blocking the vena cava, I wondered whether it was possible to remove the vena cava and not replace it. I realised it was possible. I removed the tumour and an entire segment of the inferior vena cava without reconstructing it.

Taking the time to create space, slow down, and remove myself from the distracting chatter from others and myself meant I could approach the problem with a calm mind. And standing on the opposite side and looking at the situation from a different perspective allowed me to see what I had not noticed before.

Your perspective of your experience will define the remainder of your life. You are the author of your story. In *The Power of Now*, author Eckhart Tolle argues the primary cause of unhappiness is never the situation, but our thoughts about it. Our perspective and thoughts about any of our life challenges and struggles determine how we live moving forward. If you take a different view of your cancer, you can live without fear. You can live your best life.

Reflecting on your experience, how do you want to move forward? How do you want to live? You have been given more time. You are the steward of your body and it is yours to care for. Perhaps you thought your doctors would care for you? Yes, we care about you, but your health is your responsibility. Responsibility is our 'ability' to 'respond' while owning our actions and reactions.

New choices

My patient, let's call her Maree, once said, 'I feel as if my body has betrayed me'. Perhaps you feel the same, but I ask, how have you betrayed your body and yourself? Do you smoke cigarettes? Are you spending thousands of dollars on beauty treatments to delay the appearance of ageing, yet smoke cigarettes or drink alcohol in excess or eat foods high in sugar? I'm all for beauty treatments that help you to look and feel your best. We want to look and feel well; however, no beauty treatments can counterbalance sabotaging ourselves with behaviours of unclean living.

According to the World Health Organization, obesity has doubled in the world since 1980. We now have the option of bariatric surgery, also known as metabolic surgery, which can be of great benefit in reducing weight and, for many patients, reducing or eliminating diabetes, heart disease and musculoskeletal diseases. The surgery has become popular among overweight patients.

Every surgery has risks, however, and bariatric surgery, which may include altering a person's anatomy, may result in other irreversible metabolic side effects. Many patients will regain the weight and those who do are ones who have not changed their lifestyle towards healthy living. In other words, they are still eating the wrong foods and not doing physical activity. Those patients have been sent back to the same conditions and mindset that led to their weight gain. If the root causes of a problem still exist, the problem potentially recurs.

Although, illness and cancer do occur randomly, we can make choices to support our health and our best selves. Lacking awareness of how we contribute to and manifest the very things we fear, we lose the ability to respond and take responsibility for, and to some degree control of, our wellbeing.

Saucha is another part of Niyama, the second limb of yoga, and is a practice of self-purification and cleanliness. Cleanliness can be taken in the literal sense but the practice also involves other less obvious forms of purification. Cleanliness applies to not only body hygiene, but also the foods we choose to nourish and fuel our bodies with, and even the music we listen to, the books we read, or the Netflix we binge-watch.

What do you expose your mind to? Is it positive, uplifting, thought-provoking? What thoughts do you allow to dwell in your mind? Breast surgery, chemotherapy and radiation all have associated risks, but these pale in comparison to the long-term cumulative risks of what you expose your mind and body to over many years. Remember – your behaviour has an enormous influence on your health problems, along with genetics, accessibility to health care and other factors. This means how you live, your lifestyle choices, and your attitude towards your health matters. It also means that you have control over how you choose to live your life. How good is that?!

How do you decide what you will put inside your body? When I see patients for gut problems, mostly referred to me for reflux or gallbladder disease, I question them about their diet. Most say they eat pretty healthily, and some actually do, but not all. For example, with reflux, I give patients a list of ten foods they should avoid, including things such as spicy foods and foods high in fat, coffee, alcohol and chocolate. Their response is usually the same, 'Well, doc, if I can't eat those, I can't eat anything.'

Well, there is the problem, then. If your diet consists mainly of those ten items, then it is imbalanced, and in some respects, unhealthy.

Occasionally, the gallbladder must come out when gallstones are inside and causing pain and inflammation. Afterwards, with the gallstones out or the patient on a new diet, the patient will say, 'I didn't know I could feel this good. If I had known, I would have done this years ago.' When the diet is modified, you have more energy and no longer have indigestion. But why wasn't this done years ago? The body gives you signs and symptoms. It communicates, but are you paying attention?

> **Yoga pose: Downward facing dog (ahdo mukha svanasana)**
>
> From cobra (bhujangasana) pose, tuck your toes under and, engaging your core muscles, bring your navel towards your spine. Begin to extend your tailbone towards the sky, aiming to create an inverted V with your body, hands and feet pressing into your mat. Breathe into this pose, pressing your tailbone higher and your heels towards your mat.

Taking responsibility

Taking care of your body is your responsibility. It is not your doctor's responsibility. Your doctor cannot even tell you what is wrong with you, unless you tell them what your symptoms are and why you feel the need to see a doctor. You have the responsibility to decide what nutrients will fuel your body, and how you will keep your body strong and able. My friend Jason French likens this concept to a boat. He says that the boat is the body, the captain of the boat is your emotions, but the steering wheel is your mind. The waves in the ocean are our spiritual experiences in this life. Do you want the emotion of fear dictating to your mind the direction of your boat? Your mind has the capacity to control how you live and how you choose to navigate the waves in your life. No one can do that for you. You are strong and capable. The body has an incredible resilience. Give it the support it needs by making choices that are decided by a healthy mindset. Our health begins with a healthy mind. It starts at the top.

Patients who smoke cigarettes and yet are afraid of their cancer lack insight. Although usually cancer can be treated, they are slowly killing themselves in another way. They have disconnected their behaviour from its effect on their overall health. If you are afraid of having cancer, are you not concerned about your lungs or heart?

Some have said to me, 'Well, if I'm going to die anyway, I'm going to continue to smoke.' Well, I do not know about you, but I choose to die well. I choose not to suffocate my way out of this life. Restricting the breath and suffocation is a terrible way to die. Smoking causes a slow suffocation.

However, a deeper undercurrent is present here of smoking being more than an addiction. Yes, it is a terrible addiction, but a person is also engaging in intentional self-harm. Self-care is an act of love towards yourself. How do we love others as we love ourselves, if we do not love ourselves? Only when you love yourself fully can you love others fully. What thoughts within your mind are stopping you from caring for yourself? From loving yourself? Are you not good enough or deserving of your love? Our body is a vehicle for the soul. Buddha says, 'You don't have a soul, you are a soul, you have a body.' Although, the body will one day perish, the soul does not die. Your soul is energy and consciousness. It cannot be destroyed, only transformed and, therefore, is forever. How you decide to take care of your mind and body is a personal choice, and it is your responsibility.

> **Yoga pose: Returning to mountain (tadasana)**
>
> From downward facing dog (ahdo mukha svanasana), reverse the sequence to return to mountain (tadasana) pose.
>
> On an exhale, step your feet to the top of your mat to meet your hands and move into your forward fold (uttanasana). Keep a flat, elongated spine, reaching your fingertips towards your toes as you again feel the stretch in the back body.
>
> On an inhale, roll to standing, reaching your arms overhead and keeping your shoulders away from the ears in root to rise (urdhva hastasana) pose. Find length in your spine and the side waists, while reaching your heels towards your mat. Feel the stretch in your hamstrings and calf muscles (the backs of your legs). Take your gaze upwards.
>
> Exhale and return your hands to your sides as you move back into mountain (tadasana) pose, tailbone tucked, thigh muscles engaged and length in your spine as your shoulder blades slide down your back.
>
> Notice that you were here in this same pose before. Is it the same pose? How does the body feel? Is the person doing the pose the same as before?

You can repeat the full sun salutation yoga sequence outlined through this book, continuing to notice the changes in your mind and body that make each sun salutation unique.

Mindfulness exercise: Identifying unhealthy habits

Is there a food that you enjoy eating but makes you feel unwell afterwards? Can you think of a habit that you may benefit from eliminating from your lifestyle? What one small change could you make that would benefit you mentally or physically? Take a moment to listen closely to the music you listen to often – are the lyrics positive? How does the music make you feel (angry, calm, depressed or energetic)?

CHAPTER 10

TRAINING YOUR MONKEY WITH LOVING-KINDNESS

*In the midst of movement and chaos,
keep stillness inside of you.*

DEEPAK CHOPRA

When you are in a stressful situation, the mind becomes very busy as it starts to think of the possible solutions to your problems. When you were diagnosed, your mind probably immediately wondered how you were going to work and take care of those things that you already barely got done and now had one more thing to deal with. I remember one patient whose partner was also made redundant at work and so had to continue working. Whatever your personal situation, I'm sure you have had your share of worries. The mind searches and desperately reaches for solutions and you do not sleep. You are mentally drained and physically fatigued. But you find solutions to everything. You complete your treatments. Your children are well. You juggle it all. In the case of my patient, her partner was still redundant. But because he was not working, he was available to help. The mind worries and there is endless thinking. It is important that you learn ways to rest the mind. Just as the body needs rest, the mind also needs rest. It is like a child that does not want to go to bed at night. But the moment children become calm and at peace, they fall into a much-needed sleep. The mind thinks constantly and does not stop unless you consciously help it to rest.

Training the mind to be still

The mind loves to wander, at least my mind does. My teacher says, 'A mind that cannot be controlled by its master is a dangerous mind.' Training the 'monkey mind' to focus on an object or perhaps the thoughts that run through your mind prepares your mind for meditation. Dharana, the sixth limb of yoga, is concentration. It is focused awareness and, with practice, trains the mind to be still.

I am sure you have experienced being so focused while doing an activity that you lost track of time. You were so absorbed in what you were doing that you were not aware of the happenings of your surroundings. You had a singular focus. Mostly, we are so distracted by our thoughts or the happenings around us that we do not focus. When eating, you may experience some temporary gut discomfort but dismiss it. Over time you tolerate the discomfort until it becomes your new normal. For the body to get your attention, it must awaken you with severe pain or vomiting or some other unpleasant symptom that hopefully causes you to pay attention and seek help.

When you begin practising Dharana, often the breath is used as a point of focus. It is easy and always accessible. Therefore, you can practise anywhere and anytime. Studies demonstrate that this focused practice during chemotherapy can lessen side effects of chemotherapy, particularly nausea. Concentration or stillness of the mind also allows you to integrate the principle of aparigraha, which I mention in chapter 7. (Aparigraha is the practice of non-attachment or neutrality to the outcome of our actions, and is part of Yama, the first limb of yoga.)

In the case of chemotherapy, aparigraha may mean being neutral to the experience such as nausea or the discomfort of pain, without reaction or attachment.

> **Mindfulness exercise: Candle gazing**
>
> Light a candle and sit in a quiet, dimly lit space in front of the candle. Set a timer for 10 to 15 minutes. Bring your awareness to the breath initially. Pause for a moment on the breath. Then bring your awareness to the candle. Just sit and gaze at the candle's flame. If your mind wanders, without judgement, gently bring it back to the candle flame. Continue to do this until the time has been completed. Write down how you feel. What did you notice? Write down what you observed within the candle and within yourself.

In chapter 5, I talk about the Vipassana meditation course I attended soon after I moved to Australia. It was one of the most challenging things I had ever done. My mind wandered. I created everything from meditation chairs and cushions to sit more comfortably to visions of cloud formations in the sky while sitting outside. But amazingly, I learned to be still. Eventually, my mind stopped. I could sit for three hours and allow my mind to rest, while being in awareness. What I had never realised is that our body needs to lie down and rest at night, but the mind does not necessarily rest when we sleep. It is still actively dreaming and possibly thinking. This is why you can awaken after eight hours and still feel tired. Meditation provides the mind with rest and stillness. It has been shown that a couple of hours of meditation can feel like eight hours of sleep. In early practice, it is common to fall asleep when attempting meditation – which is great if you have trouble sleeping. Meditation is a wonderful way to enter into a restful state of relaxation to prepare you for sleep.

Moving to meditation

The seventh limb of yoga is Dhyana, meditation. Dhyana is a focused awareness. A fine difference exists between Dharana (concentration) and Dhyana (meditation). And, as I mention in chapter 2, many myths are floating around about meditation too. One is that you must empty the mind of all thoughts and sit for hours in an uncomfortable position. Many methods of meditation are actually available.

The candle gazing exercise described earlier in this chapter is one form of focused meditation, where you focus on a particular object. Moving meditation is also possible – through dance, running or swimming, for example. Meditation for some may involve as little as a few minutes, or it could be several hours. You can meditate sitting in a chair, lying down, or in any other comfortable position. Meditation is possible through visualisation or chanting mantras.

Meditation is available to anyone. You don't have to go into silence for ten days to learn to meditate – although, for Vipassana practice, the ten days was necessary initially to learn this method of meditation and to still the mind. In some meditations you simply observe your thoughts, as an observer only. Interestingly, when we give our mind permission to think, the thoughts do not want to come. Prayer can also be considered a form of meditation. Meditation is for everyone, and how you access it is a very personal choice. What is certain, however, is that it is wonderful to give your mind the gift of stillness.

Yoga pose: Corpse pose (savasana)

Savasana is not part of the sun salutation sequence but is an important pose at the end of any yoga practice. Deceptively simple, it may actually be one of the most challenging and confronting poses, requiring stillness in complete awareness. In my opinion, it is one of the most important of the asanas.

Lie down on your mat with your feet wide apart, arms resting by your sides comfortably away from your body with your palms facing towards the sky. Come to a place within yourself for your final relaxation. Closing your eyes, relax your feet, legs, belly, arms, throat, face and scalp. Releasing any residual tension in your body, let go and relax every fibre of your body, but in complete awareness. Allow yourself to just be, giving yourself the gift of stillness.

Mindfulness exercise: guided meditation

Find a comfortable seated position. If you require back support, sit in a supported chair or back up against a wall. You are welcome to record the following guided meditation to play back to yourself as you move through the meditation. You may alter the script to use a language or words that resonates more with your authentic voice.

Once you have come to a seated posture, imagine a golden string descending from the sky down into your space, entering the crown of your head, running down your spine and anchoring your tailbone into your seat. Find your breath. Realise that you are breathing in and breathing out again. Allow your awareness to ride on the wave of your breath for five breaths.

Bring your attention to the toes on your right foot, then to the entire right foot. Then move your attention up to the right ankle. Pause. Move to the right calf, the right knee, and the right thigh. Focus on the entire right leg.

Now shift your awareness to the toes on the left foot, then to the entire left foot. Then move your attention up to the left ankle. Pause. Move to the left calf, the left knee, and the left thigh. Focus on the entire left leg. Then consider both of your legs.

If your mind has wandered off, gently bring your awareness back to your breath. Each time you notice your mind drifting towards thoughts, just notice this with curiosity and then gently return to the breath and the meditation.

Notice the belly, the right side, the left side, both sides and the chest. Be aware of the entire front of your torso. Shift your focus to the back of your torso. The back body. Focus on the lower back, the mid-back, the upper back, shoulder blades and shoulders. Consider the entire back body.

Now focus on the right upper arm, the right elbow and the forearm. Pause. Notice the right wrist, hand and fingers. Focus on the entire right arm and hand. Shift your awareness to your left upper arm, the left elbow and the forearm. Pause. Notice the left wrist, hand and fingers. Focus on the entire left arm and hand. Consider both arms and hands.

Shift to the throat, focusing on the jaw and an awareness of the tongue in the mouth. Notice the flow of the breath into the nostrils. Notice if the airflow is more dominant in one nostril than the other. Notice the eyelids and the eyes in the sockets. Become aware of the forehead and scalp, and the crown of the head.

Full body awareness.

Picture yourself in the space you are sitting. Hover above yourself. Move outward away from the room and see yourself within the building you are in. See yourself in the town you are in, and the region in which the town is located. See yourself in the state or province, the country that you are in. Expanding your focus outward and visualise yourself on planet Earth. The universe. And beyond and beyond and beyond that.

Now bring your focus back within the universe, picturing the planet Earth. Picture the country that you are in. The state or province. Continue to look for yourself within the region, the town or city. See yourself in the building you are in, the room where you are sitting. And see yourself there. Hover a bit longer.

Now come back into yourself, bringing the awareness back to your breath. Realise that you are breathing in and that you are breathing out. Allow your awareness to ride on the wave of your breath for a few more breaths.

Open your eyes. Take a moment to notice how you feel overall. Notice the quality of your mind. There is no right or wrong. There is only what is. Notice any thought that you have or possibly had during the meditation. If you had thoughts and your mind wandered during the meditation, congratulations for noticing them. That's a win. You were aware of the wandering and came back to your practice. Continue to practise and explore other meditation techniques as you will eventually discover one that resonates with you or possibly more than one meditation technique.

This is a forever thing

How do you feel so far in your practice? Take a moment to notice your mind and your thoughts. Notice your body. Thank yourself for coming this far, and realise all that you are capable of, without judgement.

Your journey is far from over. After completing six weeks of yoga and mindfulness training with me, one of my patients was feeling great. She had a new attitude. I told her she had two weeks of the eight-week course to go.

She told me she had noticed she could still be down some days, but she could now remind herself to cultivate the good and to just breathe. She then said the funniest thing to me: 'This is a forever thing, isn't it?'

Laughing, I replied, 'Yes, it is a practice. It doesn't end after eight weeks.'

You must continue the practice. I continue my personal practice and some days I stray from the path. With compassion, I gently come back. I do not beat myself up for not having a perfect day. I am not always Zen or Zinn in the operating room. My yoga classes are not always perfectly sequenced. I have even toppled over while teaching a pose.

To not judge yourself; there must be compassion. Practise ahimsa, part of Yama (the first limb of yoga): non-violence and compassion towards others but, most importantly, towards ourselves. It helps to have a sense of humour too. Ahimsa is a Yama that teaches us to treat others with loving-kindness, but that practice always extends to yourself as well.

CHAPTER 11

BUSY LIVING, BUSY DYING AND NO TIME FOR FEAR

It is not length of life, but depth of life.

RALPH WALDO EMERSON

Although the practice of yoga, mindfulness and meditation can create a calmness within, you will continue to have your struggles and life sufferings. But you always have a choice regarding your attitude and your response to your challenges. Let me give you an example of this.

Tracey and I met while I was living in Hawaii. She owned a kayaking tour company, and was tan, vibrant and fit. Tracey came in with a breast lump. The biopsy showed it was a cancer. She had the option to keep her breast and remove a few lymph nodes. After the initial surgery, we discussed the additional recommendations of chemotherapy and radiation. She had initially agreed to radiotherapy, but then changed her mind. She looked at me and said she was not doing chemotherapy or radiation because she didn't believe in those treatments. I advised her that her chances of the cancer returning without them would be very high. She said she would not allow herself to be ill, nauseated or fatigued. 'If I cannot live my life fully on my terms, I prefer not to live', she said.

I said, 'If the cancer returns, it may not be curable, and you could die.'

'Dr Emilia,' she said, 'I understand what I am doing. I am responsible for my decision. Will you still be my doctor?' I told her I would, even though I was not sure what I would be doing for her other than trying to convince her of getting more treatment. Eventually, I learned that it was not for me to help her, but for her to teach me.

She returned several times over months and finally a lump appeared in her armpit. 'Do you think this is cancer?' she asked.

'Yes, I do.' I answered. 'So now are you ready to consider chemotherapy? I can remove the lump and then you can still have chemotherapy. It isn't too late'.

She said, 'No, I am trying noni.' (This is a small tree that grows in the Pacific Islands, South-East Asia, Australia and India. Its leaves, fruits, roots, seeds and bark can be eaten, and these are used in traditional medicine for a number of ailments. Noni is a fix-all in Hawaii. It does have many benefits, but treating and curing advanced breast cancer is not one of them.)

Her eyes were bright with excitement as I rolled my eyes up into my head, slapping my hand across my forehead. I said, 'I know what we can do. Let's do both, noni and chemotherapy. Twice as good!' I hoped she might agree and compromise.

Again, she said, 'No, this is how I want to live my life.' With that, she danced out of my office before turning to me and saying, 'I'm going trekking in Tibet. See you next time.'

This back and forth went on for five years. Then she came in to see me on a Thursday and told me she had been to the emergency room for abdominal pain over the weekend. They had performed a CT scan. 'They said it's in my liver.' But she went on to say the pain was not that bad. She was still kayaking and working other jobs. We discussed her option of chemotherapy and I explained that it wouldn't hurt her to have a consultation and just listen and consider it. I also told her that she could start chemotherapy and that if it was as terrible as she thought she could always decide to stop. She agreed to have the consultation. As she was leaving, she invited me to play golf with her and a few mutual friends on the following Monday. I thanked her for the invite but told her, unfortunately, I had to work and could not play.

On the Tuesday morning one of our mutual friends called and announced that Tracey had died in her sleep. They had played golf the day before, laughing, eating and drinking. Tracey lived her life, her way until the very end.

Living with your consequences

Tracey taught me many lessons. Most importantly, I learned that treatment choice belongs to the patient not the doctor. I am there to educate and advise my patients of the most current relevant treatments available. I do not live with the consequences of treatment, but they do. I learned that it is a privilege to participate in another human's struggle and help them within that struggle – whether that person is family, a friend or a stranger. Tracey made me question how I prefer to live my own life. What are my terms for quality of life? She was not afraid to die; she was afraid that she would not live. As I quoted in chapter 5, Jon Kabat-Zinn said, 'He who dies before he dies, does not die when he dies'. I ask you again, how do you want to live your life?

It is a question that for some is difficult to answer. But when you are confronted with your mortality, you really give it some thought. How do you want to live the remaining days of your life? The answer is there inside of you.

For another patient of mine, let's call her Michelle, the answer was simple. She was referred to me for her newly diagnosed cancer that had already spread to her liver. She had no pain or symptoms. She was thin and looked sad and stressed. I explained that it was treatable, but not curable. However, with the most recent chemotherapies, she could possibly live for many years. I referred her on to the medical oncologist after placing a port to help with the chemotherapy. Most patients with stage 4 advanced breast cancer no longer see a surgeon, but Michelle returned a few times. On one such occasion, she asked me to complete some insurance forms, which required her to die within six months to receive payment straightaway. If she received this payment, she could stop working and afford her monthly expenses. I said, 'But you aren't going to die in six months. I don't know when you are going to die. I'm not God. I hate these forms. They are quite ridiculous. For all I know you may outlive me, and I don't even have cancer. I will complete this form, because you do have stage 4 incurable cancer, but I don't want you to believe that you are going to die in six months.'

She agreed, and said, 'I am not afraid to die'.

Your thoughts and mindset can be powerful. I have known many 'stage 4' cancer patients who live many years, much to the amazement of the medical community. They all have something in common. They believe they are going to live and are very positive. Positive thinking has been shown to attract and manifest desired outcomes. It has been demonstrated to improve stress management, improve psychological and physical wellbeing, and may increase life span. I had asked Michelle what she was going to do if she didn't work. She said she was going to work but that the job she had was stressful and she hated it. She was an artist and had always wanted to sell her art, but she wasn't sure she could make enough money to support herself. Over the passing years, Michelle has become a working artist. She is prolific, creative and full of life.

Recently, someone shared with me a Facebook post of hers. She said, 'They say I have cancer, but I feel great and my scans are all clear. Whoo hoo!' She looks alive, happy and free. I remember how she initially looked thin and defeated, with hunched shoulders. Now she looks like a different woman. And, yes, she still has 'stage 4 breast cancer' but she realises that fear and stress will not keep her alive. (It is unusual to have clear scans in advanced disease; more likely the scans showed stability or regression of disease.) Whether changes are a result of positive thinking during treatments or not, positive thinking does improve the quality of life while still alive.

You may be thinking that Michelle is going to die, regardless of her attitude. It is only a matter of time. And you are correct. She will die. You and I will die as well. The real secret (which isn't really a secret at all) is that we are all slowly dying. We do not live day to day thinking of our mortality in our conscious mind, but subconsciously for many there is fear and there is denial. But we are all ageing and slowly approaching the end of our physical existence. Despite the many benefits of positive thinking, it doesn't grant us immortality. However, it can provide a landscape in which to exist with better coping skills during times of stress and hardship, making life more joyful.

STEPS FOR DANCING IN THE DARK

So, the darkness shall be the light, and the stillness the dancing.

T.S. ELLIOT

In the beginning I asked for you to read this book slowly, preferably one chapter a week. Hopefully, you have taken your time to do the exercises and reflect over the content, and consider how it applies to you and your journey. By now, you may realise that mindfulness is a practice to be experienced and not just read from a book. This book only scratches the surface of yoga and mindfulness, to introduce you to some elements that you may want to explore further. Yoga is a life choice that provides a method through which mindfulness can be experienced.

When you begin practising yoga, you are likely not flexible or strong. Even if you are flexible, yoga will reveal areas or parts of yourself that are hard and rigid. Each time you step onto the mat is an opportunity to learn something new about yourself. As the sun rises and sets each day, each day is unique and different. Each time you do a round of sun salutation, you are different and not the same. Your feelings, thoughts and your body are unique in that instance. How wonderful it is to know that you are forever changing while on your adventure of life. It would be interesting to read this book again in a year to see if your perspective has changed again.

We all experience fear, but having a fearful mindset when no immediate threat is present causes harm to our mind and body. When diagnosed with cancer, having some amount of fear or concern for your wellbeing is normal. However, once you complete your treatment, and have given your best effort to address the problem, you must move on. It becomes a part of your past unless you continue to live it in the present. Yes, I know – what if you are stage 4 and still have cancer? You can also move on. Reread the section on acceptance back in chapter 3. Accept that you have things that you can change and things that are not within your control. The only difference between you and me is that you are more aware of what your body may die from than I am, and even then you don't really know. We are all in the same boat. Remember the saying 'get busy living or get busy dying'. Life is dynamic, not static. If your body is filled with cancer now, you are still alive. You are still evolving. Your cancer is also changing and evolving.

One of my favourite poems that my teacher, Tammy, shared with me is Rumi's 'The Guest House':

> *This being human is a guest house.*
> *Every morning a new arrival.*
>
> *A joy, a depression, a meanness, some momentary awareness comes as an unexpected visitor.*
>
> *Welcome and entertain them all!*
> *Even if they're a crowd of sorrows, who violently sweep your house empty of its furniture. Still treat each guest honorably.*
> *He may be clearing you out for some new delight.*

The dark thought, the shame, the malice, meet them at the door laughing and invite them in.

Be grateful for whoever comes, because each has been sent as a guide from beyond.

Be grateful for your struggles, challenges and even suffering. Can you make peace with your cancer as Michelle from the last chapter had? Can you acknowledge your fears, have momentary awareness of them and then let them go? There comes the time for our visiting guests to make a gracious exit. One of my friends asked me, 'Well, if you make peace with a cancer, isn't that when you die?' No, not necessarily. You are not deciding to die. On the contrary, you are choosing to live despite the struggle. This struggle or suffering is not any different from the others you have experienced, other than it has been given tremendous power.

Similarly, forgiving and making peace with the struggle is freeing. Forgiving someone or yourself does not mean you agree with what has been done, nor does it change what has occurred or the impact. It does release those involved and free you to be present and move forward. It allows what has been forgiven to be in the past. You take back your power and make a conscious choice to take back your life. Forgiveness is so empowering. Forgive yourself for not always taking care of yourself, and choose to love yourself. As author Louise Hay tells us, look at yourself in the mirror and tell yourself, 'I love you and I will take care of you.' It all starts with you.

This practice is not always easy. As I am nearing the end of writing this book, I too am struggling. I was going to put the work down for a while and leave it, until I felt better. But that would not be authentic. I feel the universe is asking me, 'But do you really believe in what you are telling your reader?' Yesterday I received a text message from a friend, a medical oncologist. He treats many breast cancer patients with chemotherapy. He is one of the most brilliant people I know. The somewhat cryptic message said, 'I will not be returning to the hospital and arrangements had been made to take care of my patients. I have received news that I did not want to hear. It is strange to sit on the other side of the desk, but that is how life is.' I was shocked and saddened to hear this.

Just a week prior another doctor that I worked with shot his wife and himself. He too had cancer and the circumstances of the murder-suicide are still unknown.

I am not feeling mindful. My mind struggles to find something positive and to make sense of these two situations. At work, staff have been asking why I am so quiet. I am processing it all. Other things are happening as well in my life and in the lives of my family and friends. It could all become overwhelming and none of it can I control or fix.

I told myself, 'You have to practise what you preach'. So, I come back to my breath. I lie down and remind myself that my friend is still alive. I remind him that he is still alive and to try to cultivate a positive mindset that will help to put him back on the other side of the desk. When he gets back there, his perspective will be changed. When he sees his patients and looks them in the eyes, he will really see them very differently, and not just their cancer. I asked him to use his challenge as an experience to make him an even greater doctor than he already is. The practice of yoga and mindfulness are not a guarantee that you will not struggle and have significant challenges. It does not make you bulletproof in this life. However, they can give you a foundation upon which you can firmly stand, lifted and able to provide light to help you and others navigate through the fog and sometimes complete darkness.

Acceptance is the critical step to facing the circumstances of what is. It pulls you in to the present. Guilt and shame are emotions derived from living in the past. Worry and fear of what is yet to come is living in the future. Neither is real. Only the moment we are in right now is real. You have no control over the past and cannot change it. You believe that you can influence your future and possibly you can, but this is only realised in retrospect in moments of reflection. You cannot change that you had cancer. You can only live as healthily as possible based on what you currently know.

When I graduated from medical school, one of my professors said, 'Knowledge is leased. The knowledge that you leave with today is based on the best that we know now. There is much more to know; therefore, you must continue your education to advance our knowledge, understanding, and contribution to the human condition.' The treatment of breast cancer has changed so much since I graduated, and this applies not just to breast cancer but also to many other disease treatments. We do not know what the future holds for breast cancer treatment. Many people live years with 'stage 4' cancer, and I believe we are on the precipice of a cure. But what if a cure is found? It would be wonderful, of course, but what would we choose to fear next? The negative chatter and doubt creep back in.

Because the reality still is that you will die of something one day and so will I. There will always be something to fear. If not this, then that. By practising the tools that you now have, you can decide how you choose to live this life that you have right now.

Letting go of those things that are not real and do not serve your higher purpose helps you to release the past. The past cannot be in the present moment, unless by choice. The past can be heavy and burdensome. Acceptance and letting go are two mindsets that go together. Holding on to past events that are pleasant creates desire, and holding on to negative memories creates aversions. Both desires and aversions cause suffering. Holding on to how life was before you had cancer is a desire that will never happen. You have changed, and would have changed anyway.

The Law of Impermanence tells us that nothing remains the same. You are not the same reader you were when you began the book. Not necessarily because of the book but because it is impossible to remain static and be alive. Everyone in your life is changing as well. Thinking that you can go back and be the same is an unrealistic illusion. Aversion leads to avoidance. One of my patients refuses to be called a 'survivor'. She is the reason I do not say survivor and instead choose to say, 'those that have experienced'. She is right, though – who wants to just survive? Nevertheless, she has aversions and fears of her cancer returning. She refuses to attend anything related to supporting breast cancer.

On the surface, it appears this is her way of letting go of breast cancer. If you have let go and have no fear, however, it does not matter whether you are at an event with other women who have experienced breast cancer, attending support groups to help other women by sharing your experience or participating in anything else related to breast cancer. She exercises to be as healthy as possible to such an extreme that she is always injured. While overcompensating, she pushes herself to the point of pain, and her body needs rest. Being healthy has a limit.

I taught yoga to triathletes and initially their intention with their practice is to increase flexibility while maintaining strength. Eventually with practice, however, they cultivate a mindset of learning to listen to their body. They suffer fewer injures, not because they are more flexible and stronger, but because they have cultivated a knowingness of their edge. They know their threshold of peak performance and when to pull back and not overtrain. You need to be able to feel when your body needs rest and nourishment. Remember to listen to what your body is telling you and provide the support it needs to be as healthy as possible. Find balance and listen to your body's wisdom. Let go and allow yourself to acknowledge what your body is communicating.

Listening to and hearing your body takes patience. Recovering not only physically, but also mentally and spiritually takes time. Allow the time you need to let yourself settle, without criticism that you are not healing as quickly as you'd prefer. You can experience the feeling of stillness and calm that arises by simply using your breath as an anchor. I believe that silence is the language of God and the universe. Be patient, slow down and create more time to hear the whisper of the Divine from within. Be without always having to do, and look for the opportunity in the moment of stillness and space. Take your time to notice that arising within you and around you, not missing a single experience and being fully alive. Practise patience with yourself and with those relationships that matter to you – your children, partner, family and friends. Loving them despite where they may be on their journey. They have their own unspoken fears of losing you. Through patience, you can accept them for who they are as you knowingly cannot change them, only love them.

Loving others as you would love yourself can be most challenging. How much do you love yourself? Developing a mindset of non-judgement begins with your feelings and thoughts about yourself. Understand that your thoughts are not always true, especially about yourself. Become an impartial witness of yourself. Who is the thinker of your thoughts? How do you develop your beliefs about anything, but especially about yourself? You are not your thoughts, nor your actions. What you have done in the past, rightfully or wrongfully, are acts or behaviours. You can choose how you want to behave now and tomorrow. Deciding how you want to treat yourself will manifest in how you treat others. We project our thoughts and beliefs onto others. For example, when someone tells you that you cannot do something, usually it is something that they cannot imagine themselves achieving. So they also believe that you could not possibly accomplish it. Only you know what you are capable of accomplishing, which is everything. Creating time and space to have an accurate understanding of yourself and others lessens the sufferings of judgement that arise from ignorance and confusion.

As you navigate the waves of your life, you usually establish goals and have dreams of the future. But fear can paralyse you. You can still dream and have goals. You can have plans without being attached to how those plans manifest. Rather, be present for each aspect of the journey. Sometimes, you may accomplish a goal, but you have already set your sights on the next, fearing that you are running out of time. This means you never really enjoy or be in the moment. Even if the moment is unpleasant, it is still an experience that should be experienced.

What lesson are you missing? Is your goal completing a treatment and just getting it over with. What did you miss? Or who did you miss? Would you want to experience anything to do with your cancer and the people you met along that journey again? In retrospect, is there something that you learned about yourself or from someone you met that would never have come into your life without the experience of cancer? Having a non-striving mindset can be a relief, as can knowing that although your eyes look forward, no matter the outcome, it will be fine. Non-striving and allowing yourself to be with the experience you are in, good or bad, frees you because you cannot fail. You do not live from a place of scarcity or lack. Know that you have all that you need to live well, without looking externally, because the source of all is within you, and you are abundantly divine.

To know this comes from experiencing it. Trust comes from within and not from external validation. Through trusting the process, despite occasional discomfort or setbacks, there is growth. You are not clinging to hope that your cancer will not recur. Alternatively, you live in the moments that you are cancer-free, shedding the burden of worry of what may or may not ever be. You have more control over the quality of your life than you appreciate. Your body and mind are brilliantly designed with the capacity to regenerate and renew. Although the body is ageing and cells are constantly turning over, it is capable of amazing things. Trust that your body can heal with the help of a healthy mindset. You can turn your health around and have a deep awareness of the gross and subtle body. After treatment is completed, the body needs loving care and support. Trust it to be able to recover fully. By taking responsibility to help yourself, you become empowered and aware, noticing what your body tells you it needs. It lets you know when it needs food and rest. Listen to and observe how your body responds to various foods, and the environment on the most subtle level. You can trust yourself and your body to guide you to optimal health.

AFTERWORD

Die happily and look forward to taking up a new and better form. Like the sun, only when you set in the west can you rise in the east.

RUMI

Perhaps it isn't hard for you to imagine the following scenario.

Come on in and have a seat. The report and biopsy confirm that your small bone lesion is from the breast cancer. The cancer has returned and is in the spine. You can see it right here on this X-ray. How are you feeling about all of this? I know that you are disappointed. You have been doing well these last several years. You have really transformed your life. Let us consider your options and then you can choose how you want to respond to this new challenge.

Now consider Anna, the patient's friend, who is angry.

'This is a load of bullshit. She has been doing yoga and meditating. She believed that if she did all those things you told her to do, including eating healthy, she would not have to deal with this anymore. It's been years and now her cancer has returned anyway.'

'I'm so sorry doc,' says the patient. 'I brought Anna because I thought it would be great for her to meet you. She is so angry, and she doesn't understand what you and I do.' Apparently, Anna has breast cancer as well. She has been living with cancer for many years. She has been on and off treatments on several occasions.

Anna says, 'I understand that you are trying to help her, grow flowers and pull weeds.'

I tell her, 'Yes, but I can see that you are angry. How does your anger serve you? Have you found it helpful?'

'Isn't this awesome?!' my patient breaks in. 'Hey, Dr Emilia, can you show Anna the breathing space exercise?'

'No, not now, I want to tell you both something.' (I want to tell you something.)

It is not constructive to seek blame for your cancer. I did not give my patient cancer. Despite the latest and greatest treatments, she will die from either cancer or something else. Anna is shocked, but that is the reality. 'What kind of doctor tells their patients they will die?' she asks. An honest one who wants her patients to live a full life without fear, based in reality. Birth and death are equally significant. One does not trump the other. They represent transitions and transformation.

I explain to my patient's friend that each day you wake up to a new day as the sun rises; it is full of potential and opportunity for you to live and make a positive impact in the lives of those you encounter. It is exciting when you realise that, each day, each of us can make a difference. We can say something or do something that creates a ripple effect, and that impact could last longer than the life that created it. Is it not what we are here to do? We do not exist without purpose; we exist to create, innovate, teach, love, learn and grow. The sun will set and as darkness falls, there is a stillness and quiet. This is a time of completion and reflection that also is welcomed. The sunrise and sunset are equally significant. One does not exist without the other. The cycle continues with this flow. Birth, death, sunrise, sunset, inhalation and exhalation, all one and the same.

Living a healthy lifestyle and practising mindfulness through yoga, meditation or any other method does not insulate you from experiencing this life and the struggles within it. Happiness does not arise because of a problem-free life, but through cultivating a mindset, perspective and awareness of the ability to respond to them. How you live and die is your choice. You can choose to be angry, unforgiving, fearful, pessimistic or cynical. Or you can choose to be kind, forgiving, grateful, hopeful and positive. You choose the quality of mind you want to carry with you through your life. You may feel a victim of your circumstances, but suffering is universal. We all get to have that experience. Cancer does not make you special. You are already special, unique and fabulous. Your lack of insight into your gifts does not mean they are non-existent. Of the seven billion people on this planet, there is only one of you. Do not waste your time fearing that which is inevitable because the universe wants you to contribute and shine your light, which will continue long after your body perishes. This is what eternal life is. The light you shine remains forever in the legacy you leave with those remaining and those who come after. Your cancer is a gift that can awaken you from the complacent slumber that many of us live. Use it to gain insight of yourself and shine brightly.

Although cancer is a scary experience, it is just an experience. You will have many more experiences in your life, some pleasant and others not so much. Being present with all experiences and seeing everything with a fresh perspective keeps you in the here and now. You are changing from moment to moment. Maintaining a beginner's mind, you can understand and be aware that you are not the same from moment to moment, despite it seeming so. You have the choice to resume your life after cancer with a renewed perspective. You can choose to live with your cancer diagnosis and be defined by it or you can use it as a springboard and leap forward into a new life.

If you still have cancer and are literally living with cancer while reading this, then do not let it rob you of your joy. You are still alive as much as I am. You are probably more present than most people. It may be easier to feel the here and the now. To see each moment for what it is, while leaving the superficial aspects of life behind. You are more alive than the rest of us who may struggle to appreciate every moment. As the body may slow and deteriorate over time with ageing, the mind does not have to. You can continue to be keenly aware because the soul or consciousness does not age.

Well, if you have a regular yoga and meditation practice (or remember back to chapter 1 when I introduced the eight limbs of yoga), you may be wondering, 'Yeah, but what about the last limb of yoga?! You only have written about seven of them. What about Samadhi?' Well, yes, you are correct. I have not mentioned it. Patañjali describes eight limbs of yoga, and the eighth and final limb is Samadhi. The practice of all other limbs which ultimately help to experience Samadhi, defined as a state of meditative absorption where, through the practice of concentration and effortless meditation, you come to understand the truth without distorted commentary from the mind. There are several types of Samadhi. Some have said that experiencing Samadhi is not a destination but the beginning of yoga – because yoga means union. Union of the mind, body and spirit. Yoga can also mean to yoke or to harness – harnessing the mind. The practice can also lead to what some would call enlightenment, or a state of bliss. I believe it is seeing the true nature of yourself and all beings. When we end our yoga practice on the mat, we bring our hands together at our heart centre, like in prayer, and say 'Namaste'. It is intentional that the hands come to the heart. The heart is the seat of our soul. We take the moment to acknowledge what we see within ourselves and bow to one another, acknowledging that we see the true nature of ourselves in each other. I am saying to you that I see you and I see you within myself. It is also in some cultures used as a greeting. To be seen and accepted without judgement as our authentic self is something that we all truly desire. This doesn't mean being validated by someone else, but is about being seen despite the external superficial differences. I see you! I love you as I love myself.

I have only experienced brief glimpses of what I feel is Samadhi. Integrating the other limbs of yoga into one union takes continuous disciplined practice. Once I was experimenting with open-eyed meditation. I was on the beach and there were plenty of distractions. One moment a dog was running past, the next children were playing, and then a surfer carrying his board. I took the time to appreciate the cool breeze on my skin, providing relief from the heat of the sun. I acknowledged the sounds of laughter, birds flying overhead and the waves crashing and subsiding into a thin white foam over the wet sand. My focus became more and more narrowed as I noticed the smallest grains of sand blown by the sea breeze. What happened next, I had never experienced. I felt as if everything disappeared, including myself, but I was conscious and aware. In that moment, I realised that everything is me and I am everything. I am great, significant and powerful, and I am also small, nothing, a grain of sand. It was a great feeling and I could have just stayed there. My mind was calm. I was not creating anything or thinking. My breath was shallow. My body felt free, and lighter – just pure energy and awareness.

We know that energy is never destroyed, only transformed. If we are energy and our consciousness can never be destroyed and transformed, then there is no room for holding onto fear, especially the fear of becoming non-existent and forgotten. We become transformed. I felt lighter and relieved, as if a burden had been lifted. This is what Samadhi felt like to me. Although this feeling was brief, I knew that I could practise and experience it again. It is a place within that is always there and always has been.

Afterwards, I felt from my heart a knowing that we are all connected. What I do to others, I do to myself. If I want to be free and feel unconditional love from others, I must love myself and others unconditionally. I am not an expert on Samadhi, and it is my hope that through my continued practice that I will have more experiences with this feeling and for longer periods of time.

It is my hope for you that you will have enough interest to explore yoga and all the limbs further, and have your own personal experiences that will lead you to your freedom and knowingness from an inner wisdom that has been within you from your beginning – a knowingness that we are all one consciousness. A knowingness that all will be well, with me, with you and with us all.

Lokah Samastah Sukhino Bhavantu: may all beings be happy and free, and may the thoughts, words and actions of my own life contribute in some way to that happiness and freedom for you and for all.

Namaste and amen.

KEY TERMS

Anicca: The Law of Impermanence; all things change

Mindfulness: Paying attention on purpose without judgement

Neuroplasticity: The ability of the brain to create new neural pathways

Sankalpa: Intention, committed vow

Yoga: To unite or yoke; a practice of living

The limbs of yoga

The limbs of yoga are the eight aspects of yoga practice, described by Patañjali:

- Yama: The first limb of yoga; disciplines of how to treat others:
    - Ahimsa: First yama or discipline; non-violence or compassion
    - Satya: Second yama; honesty
    - Asteya: Third yama; non-stealing
    - Brahmacharya: Fourth yama; right use of energy
    - Aparigraha: Fifth yama; non-attachment or non-hoarding

- Niyama: The second limb of yoga; observances of how to treat yourself:
  - Saucha: First niyama or observance; purity or cleanliness
  - Santosa: Second niyama; contentment
  - Tapas: Third niyama; fiery discipline
  - Svadhyaya: Fourth niyama; self-inquiry or self-study
  - Isvara pranidhana: Fifth niyama; surrendering to that which is greater than oneself
- Asana: The third limb of yoga; the physical practice of yoga, the poses or postures
- Pranayama: The fourth limb of yoga; breathing and different aspects of breath work or exercises
- Pratyahara: The fifth limb of yoga; withdrawal of senses
- Dhyana: The sixth limb of yoga; focused concentration
- Dharana: The seventh limb of yoga; meditation
- Samadhi: The eighth limb of yoga; bliss or enlightenment

The pillars of mindfulness

Acceptance

Letting go

Patience

Non-striving

Non-judgement

Trust

Beginner's mind

REFERENCES AND RECOMMENDED READING

The following is a list of books mentioned throughout this book, as well as some of my favourites that I found enjoyable to read and insightful.

Albom, Mitch, 1997, *Tuesdays with Morrie*, Doubleday

Brown, Brené, 2012, *Daring Greatly*, Penguin

Chopra, Deepak, 1992, *Unconditional Life*, Bantum Books

Frankel, Viktor, 2011, *Man's Search for Meaning*, Rider

Goenka, S.N., 2014, *The Art of Dying*, Vipassana Research Publications

Goenka, S.N., 2014, *Vipassana Meditation: The Art of Living*, Vipassana Research Publications

Hanson, Rick, 2014, *Hardwiring Happiness*, Penguin

Hay, Louise, 2006, *The Power is within You*, Hay House

Hay, Louise, 2004, *You Can Heal Your Life*, Hay House

Iyengar, B.K.S., 2008, *Light on Life*, Rodale

Kabat-Zinn, Jon, 2005, *Wherever You Go, There You Are*, Hachette Books

Kalanithi, Paul, 2016, *When Breath Becomes Air*, Random House

Millman, Dan, 2000, *Way of the Peaceful Warrior*, H.J. Kramer

Pausch, Randy, 2008, *The Last Lecture*, Hyperion

Tolle, Eckhart, 2004, *The Power of Now*, Namaste Publishing

Williamson, Marianne, 1992, *A Return to Love*, Harper Collins

Yogananda, Paramhansa, 2007, *The Essence of the Bhagavad Gita*, Crystal Clarity Publishers

ACKNOWLEDGEMENTS

Sir Isaac Newton once said, 'If I have seen further it is by standing on the shoulders of giants.' I am grateful for the giants who have lifted me.

I am who I am today because of the sacrifices of my mother, Martha Dauway. She believed in me before I believed in myself, and I am eternally grateful for her wisdom and unconditional love.

To my sister, Terri, whose experience with breast cancer provided perspective for how I should care for patients, and to Toni, my sister, who is selfless and always a phone call away to advise and mentor me: I love you both.

Paul, you unknowingly brought me back to my mat by teaching me the philosophy of yoga. I hope you will continue to dream big. Tammy, my yoga teacher and mentor, thank you for bringing me back to my mat when I stray from it and always reminding me the true meaning of yoga while encouraging me to always ask, 'Is this action aligned with my higher purpose?'

Sally, my McGrath Breast Care nurse, I thank you for your genuine care of all the patients we have shared, and for your objective feedback of this book and your friendship.

Kareen, for sharing your feelings and thoughts, and for reading this book and providing insights into the mindset of a patient's journey.

Denise White, my unofficial editor, for taking the time to read the initial manuscript and providing honest criticism with great humour.

Charlotte, my editor and a secret yogi whose personal practice of yoga helped me to deliver this message with clarity and compassion: I hope to work together again.

For my surgical colleagues who have shared their knowledge and skills, 'As iron sharpens iron', so too have you sharpen me.

And to my patients, who have been my greatest teachers, I thank you for your courage, sharing your life stories, and the privilege to participate in your journey.

AUTHOR BIO

Dr Emilia Dauway, MD, FACS, FRACS, is the former Chief of Breast Surgery and Director of the Breast Cancer Program at Baylor, Scott and White Healthcare in Texas, USA. She is a graduate of the Johns Hopkins University (1987) and the University of Illinois, College of Medicine (1992). After completing her internship and residency in general surgery at the Ochsner Clinic (1997), she completed a fellowship in surgical oncology at Moffitt Cancer Institute at the University of South Florida (1999) including specialised training in breast surgery.

She has now taken the opportunity to practice general, breast and oncologic surgery in Australia. As a member of the Breast Surgeons of Australia New Zealand and the American Society of Breast Surgeons, she is an expert in the treatment of breast disease. She gained recognition as a Fellow of the Society of Surgical Oncology in 2000, a Fellow of the American College of Surgeons in 2002 and Fellow of the Royal Australasian College of Surgeons in 2016.

Dr Dauway also identified a need to educate regional women regarding current breast cancer treatment options, especially in the areas of breast preservation and reconstruction after mastectomy. She believes that all women should have the same treatment options, survival advantages and quality of life, regardless of geographical location. She founded Restore More, a non-profit organisation that provides education to empower women to make better health treatment decisions. RESTORE More's latest projects include providing a breast screening clinic and breast prostheses to women in Nepal.

As a trained yoga and mindfulness instructor, she incorporates mindfulness and restorative yoga techniques into her surgical practice, to help those who have experienced breast cancer live a quality life after treatment through mindful living.

She has worked with medical missions internationally in Peru, Nicaragua, El Salvador, Haiti, Paraguay, and Cameroon, Africa. Dr Dauway was awarded 'Inspirational Woman of the Year 2019', for her holistic approach to surgery and her work with regional women through RESTORE More.

A portion of the proceeds from *Live Fearlessly* will be donated to RESTORE More.

www.ingramcontent.com/pod-product-compliance
Lightning Source LLC
Chambersburg PA
CBHW050317010526
44107CB00055B/2276